Report to the United States Congress

The 2004 National Export Strategy

The Administration's Trade Promotion Agenda
Unlocking America's Potential

Trade Promotion Coordinating Committee
Donald L. Evans, Chairman

Contents

Letter from the Secretary of Commerce

Dear Mr. President and Mr. Speaker:

As Chairman of the Trade Promotion Coordinating Committee (TPCC), it is my privilege to present to you the National Export Strategy. Three years ago, the TPCC agencies committed themselves to implementing a set of recommendations based on direct input from our customers and an analysis of the programs of our most competitive foreign trading partners. As part of the President's Management Agenda, the TPCC agencies did a thorough stocktaking of their programs and services with the goals of becoming more responsive to their clients and of adopting best practices.

We have achieved a great deal to be proud of and have a new commitment to continuous management improvement of our programs and services. Having fulfilled the objectives we set out to accomplish in the 2002 National Export Strategy Report, the TPCC agencies are ready to take a forward-looking approach and use our trade promotion programs more strategically. The TPCC agencies will do so by closely coordinating their efforts in support of major Administration priorities to enable American businesses, workers, and farmers to succeed in the global marketplace and by playing a critical role in strengthening new democracies.

The TPCC has identified three areas where the participation of U.S. exporters and investors will be essential to that effort:

- Continuing implementation of the Administration's 2002 National Export Strategy and the trade promotion recommendations found in the January 2004 report, *Manufacturing in America*;

- Follow-up by U.S. businesses in markets where we have recent or pending free trade agreements; and

- Support of the Administration's national economic security agenda in countries that have suffered debilitating crises, such as Iraq and Afghanistan.

We know that our companies are competing in a global market where foreign competition is fierce. Providing them with the right tools and leveling the playing field are hallmarks of our efforts. Where our foreign competitors rely on inappropriate, unfair, or market-distorting practices, we are responding to these situations aggressively through our trade laws, our compliance efforts, and through negotiations within international organizations. Especially in the context of this extremely competitive environment, we want to make sure that our companies have world-class trade promotion and finance services and are in the best possible position to enter and successfully compete in today's global marketplace.

Implementation of the 2002 Recommendations

Since the release of the 2002 National Export Strategy, all of the core agencies have made significant progress implementing the Report's recommendations. The agencies have developed initiatives to respond directly to this Administration's strategic priorities, and in some cases have implemented significant programmatic and organizational reforms. As a result, our trade promotion programs are more responsive to the customer.

Major achievements over the last three years include:

- **A renewed focus on the customer through agency reorganizations.** Within the Department of Commerce's International Trade Administration (ITA), we laid the groundwork for the consolidation of all export promotion—including outreach, client management, project development, and company problem solving—with the enactment of Public Law (P.L.) 108-199. This reorganization will build greater synergies between the Advocacy Center and the Commercial Service's field operations. At the Export-Import Bank of the United States (Ex-Im Bank), all financing products are now housed in one place, with an emphasis on reducing processing time. The Overseas Private Investment Corporation (OPIC) has created a new Small Business Center with one-stop shopping for small- and medium-sized companies.

- **Co-guarantee arrangement between Ex-Im Bank and the Small Business Administration (SBA).** When implemented, this arrangement will allow a lender (and the exporter) to move seamlessly between SBA and Ex-Im Bank when SBA's guaranty limit is reached. SBA provides a co-guarantee for an amount up to its guarantee limit and Ex-Im Bank will provide a co-guarantee for the remainder of the loan. The advantage for the client is that it only has to deal with one entity: SBA handles the back-office operations and facilitates Ex-Im Bank's review.

- **Early project development.** TPCC agencies have identified possible project opportunities in Mexico. In Brazil, we have identified priority infrastructure projects under Brazil's Public-Private Partnership. In Russia, we are focusing on infrastructure and transportation security projects. Under ITA's reorganization, we are placing the Advocacy Center within the Commercial Service. This change will increase synergies between Ex-Im Bank and the Commercial Service's overseas field operations. We are also marketing Ex-Im Bank Letters of Interest with the Commercial Service's foreign posts.

Mixed credit initiative. Our mixed credit initiative enables the Agency for International Development (USAID) to combine its grants with Ex-Im Bank loans and guarantees for developmental, non-commercially viable projects. Agencies are now putting together a mixed credit for a rural electrification project in Guatemala.

FEED (front-end engineering and design) studies. Shortly after the U.S. Trade and Development Agency (USTDA) agreed to finance FEED studies, Japanese negotiators at the Organization for Economic Cooperation and Development (OECD) committed to stop the practice of providing tied FEED studies when the follow-on project is untied.

Greater awareness of interagency programs. We have trained nearly 100 TPCC agency staff from 10 different agencies to be fully aware of the range of products and services for small businesses available throughout the government. Most of the agencies have contributed financially to this training module, and because feedback from participants has been excellent, it is likely the training will become permanent. As more staff are trained in the key features of other agency programs and the needs of small companies throughout the export and investment process, the agencies will be better equipped to guide small businesses through "the maze" of available export promotion services.

State and local outreach—California. The State of California is considering a TPCC proposal developed by the Commercial Service that builds on long-standing successful collaboration among the Departments of State, Agriculture, and Commerce. Under the proposal, the TPCC agencies would partner with the state to provide export promotion and finance services. State budget cutbacks have forced the closure of state services in this area. The Federal Government can provide these services, and in some cases obviate the need for state funding.

Marketing. A TPCC export pavilion that is used at major trade shows has replaced ad hoc efforts on the part of the agencies. Funded jointly by a number of TPCC agencies, the pavilion is now in high demand by trade show organizers, who offer free space to encourage our participation.

Export.gov. All of the TPCC agencies now share one export-focused portal on the Internet. For those exporters who register, their information is automatically used to populate many TPCC agency export-related forms. Additional forms are continually being added.

Trade Policy Agenda

Three years ago, the Administration initiated a plan for the United States to pursue reinforcing free trade initiatives globally, regionally, and bilaterally. With bipartisan support for the passage of Trade Promotion Authority by Congress in 2002, the Administration has put that authority to good use in 2003—playing a leadership role in the World Trade Organization (WTO), making progress toward a Free Trade Area of the Americas (FTAA), completing state-of-the-art free trade agreements (FTAs) with Chile and Singapore, launching free trade negotiations with 12 more nations, announcing its intention to begin free trade negotiations with eight additional countries, and putting forward regional trade strategies in Southeast Asia and the Middle East. With five FTAs in place or imminently in place and many more FTAs in the works, we are now developing government-wide commercial strategies that assist U.S. companies in taking full advantage of these agreements.

These efforts include:

- **China export promotion strategy.** A China export promotion strategy that elevates our level of cooperation under the U.S.-China Joint Commission on Commerce and Trade. This strategy will focus our promotional efforts on our most promising opportunities;

- **Commercial strategies for FTA countries.** Development of commercial strategies that follow through on recently negotiated FTAs. For each FTA, we have identified the sectors that have the best opportunities for the year, developed an outreach strategy to ensure U.S. companies in these sectors learn about the opportunities, and targeted TPCC agency programs and services in a strategic fashion to ensure that U.S. companies are well positioned to make sales in these markets. Significantly, a process has been developed that can be applied to future FTAs.

Focus on Manufacturing

Our goal now must be to build on the policy accomplishments and programmatic achievements of the past three years. With an improved set of trade promotion and finance tools now in place, the TPCC agencies must put these programs to work, especially for U.S. small businesses.

The Administration's Manufacturing Initiative, which was announced in March 2003, will reinforce this effort. Our January 2004 report, _Manufacturing in America: A Comprehensive Strategy to Address the Challenges to U.S. Manufacturing,_ presents a comprehensive set of recommendations that respond directly to challenges identified by U.S. manufacturers in more than 20 nationwide roundtables that included a broad mix of small, medium, and large companies. This is similar to the approach the TPCC took when it based its 2002 Report on recommendations from nationwide surveys and meetings with exporters.

In these roundtables, individual manufacturers stressed a number of issues centering on domestic economic and regulatory policy. But they also focused extensively on issues relating to international trade. They emphasized the importance of breaking down the barriers that other governments erect against U.S. exporters and eliminating the practices that distort trade and investment. They stressed that U.S. foreign economic policy should ensure that competition is free and fair. And they emphasized the need to strengthen U.S. trade promotion efforts in markets opened by recent trade agreements, particularly in China.

Manufacturing in America contains several recommendations related to the TPCC that we are implementing, including: accelerating implementation of the 2002 National Export Strategy and consolidating the export promotion functions of the Commerce Department to enhance U.S. Government efforts on behalf of U.S. manufacturing. In addition, _Manufacturing in America_ calls on the TPCC to develop a joint public-private global supply chain initiative to promote more global opportunities for small and medium-sized manufacturers.

Supply Chain. In their comments at the manufacturing roundtables, smaller U.S. manufacturers expressed concern that they were under pressure to move their operations offshore as manufacturers to whom they sold their products moved offshore. The companies felt they could better cope with these pressures if they had improved access to foreign companies' supply chains. Over the next six months, TPCC agencies, along with staff of the Commercial Service, the new Manufacturing and Services unit of ITA, and key partners in the private sector, will work to craft a set of programs and services to help small- and medium-sized manufacturers obtain access to global supply

---

**Success Story:
SBA Helps Small Business Tap
Global Supply Chains**

Semi-Bulk SystemS, Inc. (SBS) of Fenton, Missouri, has been doing international business for over 17 years, often dealing with large international companies or with the foreign subsidiaries of Fortune 500 companies. Recently, SBS used the Small Business Administration's Export Working Capital Program to support contracts with several large international companies throughout Europe for projects requiring SBS's sanitary systems for the manufacture of ice cream. Building on these contracts, SBS hopes to expand its business to other international companies and subsidiaries of U.S. companies in the sanitary and industrial process industries.

chains of multinational companies, both overseas and in the United States. As a first step, we will develop sector case studies to assess the nature of supply chains, and we will evaluate gaps that remain by interviewing large and small domestic companies, as well as foreign producers.

Economic Security Agenda

Over the last two to three years, the TPCC has become an increasingly effective tool for furthering the Administration's national economic security agenda in countries that have suffered debilitating crises. In order to achieve greater global and economic security, we have to be able to foster economic growth, strengthen emerging democracies, create new jobs, and build strong trading partnerships in countries such as Iraq and Afghanistan. Private-sector development is the key to stimulating the growth needed for stability and job creation. The important role of the TPCC agencies is to encourage the U.S. private sector to take an interest and have a stake in the future of post-crisis countries. Bringing U.S. companies with their capital and know-how into these markets does more than fund critical projects and infrastructure, such as hospitals and hotels. It also introduces these economies to the success of America's innovation and ethical business standards and practices.

In past crisis situations, American industry was ready and willing to play a role in the rebuilding of shattered economies—but it was hampered by uncoordinated government efforts. We have improved our ability to quickly provide U.S. companies with the information and support they need to be the catalyst for growth in fragile economies. In countries like Iraq, entrepreneurialism is now on the rise. With the help of U.S. companies, these countries can stand as examples of the benefits of democracy and free markets to oppressed people everywhere.

   Coordination in post-crisis regions. We will continue our efforts on a government-wide approach to reconstruction of Iraq and Afghanistan and develop initiatives to encourage the private sector to take a stake in the future of post-crisis economies.

Conclusion

The TPCC agencies are on the right path and are focused on continuous program coordination and improvement in order to best serve America's businesses. We have streamlined bureaucracies, and made our programs more responsive, efficient, and easier to use. Small businesses and manufacturers have more resources devoted to gaining access to markets in China, free trade agreement countries such as Chile and Singapore, and with Australia, the Central American countries, and Morocco. At the same time, we are using all of our trade promotion tools to support our national security agenda. The TPCC is committed to creating the jobs that flow from trade. Under the Administration's leadership, the TPCC will continue to meet the goals of the national export strategy and contribute to the success of America's businesses and entreprenueurs.

Sincerely,

Donald L. Evans
Secretary of Commerce and
Chairman of the Trade Promotion Coordinating Committee

Status of 2002 Recommendations: New Tools and Better Service

Customer Service:
Agency Restructuring Efforts to Meet Client Needs

Three years ago, the Trade Promotion Coordinating Committee (TPCC) agencies committed themselves to ensuring that U.S. exporters, particularly small- and medium-sized enterprises (SMEs), have access to world-class trade promotion services. We listened to exporters first—through extensive surveys and focus groups—before deciding what to do. The overwhelming message was that while exporters are generally satisfied with our existing programs, they need state-of-the-art programs and services in order to compete in the twenty-first century. Time is as important as money when it comes to pursuing foreign market opportunities—making customer service a necessity, not a luxury.

That message has reverberated within the core agencies of the TPCC. It has strengthened the TPCC's emphasis on small businesses—the engines of growth and jobs in America. Reform efforts at three agencies—the Export-Import Bank of the United States (Ex-Im Bank), the Overseas Private Investment Corporation (OPIC), and the U.S. Department of Commerce—have grown in scope from adding specific programs and services to overhauling agencies' organizational structures and client management practices.

Export-Import Bank

Early in FY 2003, Ex-Im Bank undertook a reorganization aimed at making itself more market-focused and customer-driven while enhancing risk management. Major changes involved the creation of a unified Export Finance group devoted to managing transaction relationships across all Ex-Im Bank financing products and the creation of an independent Credit and Risk Management group to provide consistent credit standards and oversight. Ex-Im Bank designed this results-oriented program in response to the challenge put forth by President Bush in his vision for management reform.

The reorganization has focused on a reduction of transaction processing times. Producing final credit decisions more quickly and predictably has involved cultural, procedural, and staffing changes. To assist in identifying additional areas for process changes that would improve performance, Ex-Im Bank engaged a process engineering team. Ex-Im Bank has implemented a number of the team's recommendations and expects to make further progress in FY 2004.

Overseas Private Investment Corporation

In 2003, OPIC continued its strong commitment to creating new investment opportunities for small U.S. businesses. Following up on last year's Small Business Initiative with the Small Business Administration (SBA) and the creation of an OPIC Small Business Center (SBC) focusing on businesses with annual revenues of less than $35 million, this year OPIC created a Small and Medium Enterprise Department.

Success Story: Teamwork Helps Trading Company Grow Into a Manufacturer

Four years ago, MAS Exports Ltd.'s (MAS) bank decided it would no longer support small export transactions, including MAS's $250,000 export working capital line of credit. A bank representative, who was also a member of the local District Export Council (private partners of the federal agencies), helped set MAS up with the SBA and the Small Business Assistance Corporation (SBAC) in Savannah, Georgia, which in turn found a new bank for MAS. The new bank, First National Bank and Trust of Statesboro, Georgia, had never extended an export line of credit before. But after training in export financing and SBA programs, the bank approved its first export working capital line of credit with MAS.

SBA then referred MAS to the local Commerce Department office in Savannah to help the company strengthen its business plan by expanding its foreign customer base beyond mainly a single foreign buyer. With the help of the Commerce Department, MAS soon expanded its client base from Jamaica to several other countries. MAS then began working with the automotive team of the Sunbelt U.S. Export Assistance Center, made up of the Commerce Department; the Georgia Department of Industry, Trade and Tourism (GDITT); SBA; and the Small Business Development Center (SBDC) of the University of Georgia. Over the last two years, MAS has attended the automotive trade show in Las Vegas with the Georgia team to meet with foreign buyers brought to the show by the Commerce Department's International Buyer Program. MAS's participation was made possible by GDITT's help with costs associated with the event.

With the resulting export sales, MAS's export working capital line has grown to $500,000, and the company has obtained Ex-Im Bank credit insurance on its receivables. With sales growing steadily to $1,000,000 as a trading company, MAS recently made the tentative decision to go into production of lubricant products for itself. The SBAC and SBDC helped MAS develop projections for moving to production and hiring new employees. The bank, as one of SBA's Preferred Lenders, has approved a $250,000 International Trade Loan to purchase the necessary equipment.

As MAS makes the transition from a trading company to a new small manufacturing company, it appears that they have taken all the right steps, including hard work and dedication and benefiting from the assistance of nearly all of the federal and state export assistance partners along the way. In addition, MAS's bank, First National Bank and Trust, is now expanding in southeast Georgia and is interested in doing other export deals.

This department is responsible for OPIC's Direct Loan program, which provides financing to U.S. SMEs with annual revenues of less than $250 million. In addition, the SBC has been aligned with this new department, providing streamlined, "one-stop shopping" for small- and medium-sized businesses seeking OPIC services for investment overseas. OPIC remains committed to reduced processing cycle time and streamlined application support requirements.

These structural changes have borne results. In 2003, through diligent efforts, 42 of OPIC's 73 committed projects were for SMEs. Seventy-three percent of these projects were completed through the Small Business Center. Efforts are under way to build a robust pipeline of additional transactions for the current fiscal year. These projects include the expansion of an airline in the Caucasus region by a U.S. small business group, helping a California company to provide a nutritional drink in Central America, and helping a Florida company expand Internet security in Latin America.

In order to increase public awareness and understanding of OPIC's programs and activities with a particular focus on the small business community, OPIC has launched a new Partners Program with trade councils, business associations, and foreign policy organizations nationwide.

State Department

The State Department, leading the commercial function in some 110 diplomatic posts where the Commerce Department does not currently operate, has launched efforts to strengthen Washington-based coordination of its commercial advocacy work, which incorporates Administration goals and initiatives. Under its Business Facilitation Incentive Fund, State has sharpened the criteria for funding strategic commercial advocacy initiatives undertaken by these non-Commercial Service overseas posts. Beyond its traditional advocacy and market access agenda, State has initiated a number of projects directed at improving the climate for U.S. business, building public-private partnerships that can help open new markets, and encouraging best business practices and corporate social responsibility.

Commerce Department:
International Trade Administration

With Congress' passage of the omnibus spending bill in January 2004, the International Trade Administration (ITA) embarked on a landmark reorganization. The last time ITA was reorganized, U.S. exports totaled $282 billion and imports were only $303 billion; trade with Mexico totalled $20 billion; and there were no Internet companies. Now, U.S. imports and exports are above the trillion-dollar mark, and trade with Mexico is over $200 billion. In fact, we now engage in more trade with developing economies than all our trade (with developed and developing countries) back then. And we have tens of thousands of information technology companies.

How ITA Will Change

All four program-focused business units will be affected by the reorganization.

All trade promotion programs will join the Commercial Service (including the Trade Information Center [TIC], the Advocacy Center, the Central and Eastern Europe Business Information Service [CEEBIC], and the Business Information Service for the Newly Independent States [BISNIS]) under the renamed Assistant Secretary for **Trade Promotion (TP)** and Director General for the U.S. and Foreign Commercial Service.

The reorganization replaces Trade Development with an Assistant Secretary for **Manufacturing and Services (MAS)**. The new unit will take on the responsibility of evaluating the impact of domestic and international economic policies on U.S. manufacturing and services and will work with other U.S. Government agencies in developing a public policy environment that enhances U.S. industry competitiveness.

Market Access and Compliance (MAC) will establish a new working relationship with the Commercial Service to broaden its capability to monitor and address compliance issues.

Import Administration (IA) will develop improved instruments for combating unfair trade. IA will increase its focus on China.

An important element of the reorganization is the creation of a new position, Assistant Secretary for Manufacturing and Services. An equally important outcome will be the consolidation of all ITA trade promotion functions within the Commercial Service unit. This realignment will generate new synergies and coordination of outreach, marketing, client management, project development, and company problem solving. It will also make ITA a more focused and effective partner within the TPCC.

More than just a streamlining of resources, the reorganization will strengthen ITA's focus on customer service. Previously, ITA's trade promotion functions were scattered throughout the operating units, each with its own client databases, computer systems, and marketing strategies. With the reorganization, the Commercial Service will be fully empowered and accountable for trade promotion and client services. This will be accomplished through:

- Strengthened information management and outreach: integration of the Trade Information Center (TIC) and the regional business centers (BISNIS and CEEBIC) into the Commercial Service's overseas and domestic networks.

- More strategic and available advocacy services: integration of the Advocacy Center with the Commercial Service's overseas network to provide more focused early project development support, tighter linkages with the domestic network to improve outreach to the SME community, and an important hub for the trade finance agencies within ITA.

- Better integration of agreements compliance services and enforcement within ITA and with other Federal Government agencies.

- A country-by-country strategic planning process linking policy and promotion.

Small Business Finance

Ex-Im Bank/SBA Harmonization: Co-guarantee Initiative

Ex-Im Bank and SBA will create a co-guarantee agreement that builds on previous efforts to harmonize the export working capital loan programs of both agencies. The goal is to make financing available to small businesses in a more seamless manner. Currently, if an SBA lender needs a guarantee for a working capital loan above SBA's limit, the lender has the options of switching its relationship to Ex-Im Bank (which has no limit), abandoning the transaction, or obtaining an SBA guarantee at a lower percentage cover. The intent of the co-guarantee is to bridge the gap between SBA's guarantee limit and the size of lending that most small business exporters would need to attract interest from lenders who use Ex-Im Bank's Export Working Capital Guarantee Program. The co-guarantee will allow SBA lenders to continue to work through their SBA relationship to obtain working capital guarantees for export-related loans. Of the 90 percent guaranteed amount, SBA will provide a co-guarantee up to its loan limit, and Ex-Im Bank will provide a co-guarantee for the remainder.

Greater coordination of SBA's and Ex-Im Bank's Export Working Capital Programs will result in a seamless process for facilitating necessary funding for small businesses. This approach will provide the exporter with more easily accessible trade finance and the lender with combined SBA and Ex-Im Bank coverage without having to deal with two separate agencies. While both agencies will need to approve each credit, SBA will have sole authority to approve servicing and liquidation actions under the co-guarantees.

Success Story: Ex-Im Bank Helps Small Manufacturer Expand Export Sales

With 35 employees, Bio-Lok of Deerfield Beach, Florida, is a manufacturer and distributor of dental implants sold to other distributors, who in turn sell to clinicians. In addition to its three foreign subsidiaries, Bio-Lok has distribution agreements with entities in 12 countries worldwide. The company manufactures and distributes the Micro-Lok™ and Silhouette Precision Dental Implant Systems consisting of dental implants, related prosthetics, devices, tools, spade drills, and items purchased for resale.

The company suffered a series of misfortunes, including two bankruptcies. After emerging from Chapter 11 in 1996, Bio-Lok initiated a merger, introduced new products, and improved manufacturing techniques. Then, in July 2001, a fire stalled production and marketing for eight weeks. The company quickly replaced machinery and equipment with the help of insurance proceeds, but continued to suffer quarterly losses due to these setbacks.

Then the Florida Export Finance Corporation helped Bio-Lok complete an Ex-Im Bank application for a $2 million Revolving Working Capital Guarantee. In November 2002, Commercebank in Florida approved a loan that has since supported $2.5 million in export orders. Bio-Lok anticipates increasing its domestic staff and adding distributors in Asia, Europe, and South and Central America. Buoyed by the introduction of its new Laser-Lok Implant, the company continues to build marketing and expects to be marginally profitable again in 2004, supported by exports that in the first quarter of 2004 were up 9 percent. Exports remain a strategic building block for the future.

OPIC-SBA Cooperation

SBA and OPIC recognize that increased cooperation between them will serve their common objectives and missions, including the delivery of services to U.S. small businesses interested or involved in international trade. SBA and OPIC are working together to (1) strengthen institutional ties and share general information, (2) develop cross-training programs for SBA and OPIC staff, and (3) initiate a coordinated outreach and marketing effort to reach more small businesses. Their joint goal is to increase the number and dollar value of U.S. small business exports.

Early Project Development

A key finding in TPCC interviews with U.S. exporters was that foreign companies often have a competitive advantage before a project or procurement reaches the tender stage. Often, U.S. companies are shut out of potential competitions early in the project concept, at the pre-qualification, or at the pre-tender stage. This advantage of some foreign companies is attributed to the long-term commitment of their national governments to develop projects in strategically important emerging markets and strong linkages between foreign governments and their private companies.

Leveling the Playing Field

The U.S. Government's trade-related agencies are committed to providing U.S. exporters the same level of strategic, coordinated support that foreign governments routinely provide their companies in pursuit of foreign business opportunities. The intent is to harness agencies' efforts early in the deal-making process in order to present a more aggressive posture vis-à-vis the competition. Specific aims are (1) to identify nascent

---

Foreign Competitor Practices

The TPCC's early project development initiative seeks to level the playing field for U.S. exporters by competing at the same level as foreign governments that try to give their respective companies a "jump" on the competition. Practices the TPCC hopes to counter include:

Early Finance Support: Foreign governments influence projects to suit their interests through early expressions of available financing. U.S. exporters believe early export credit agency (ECA) support is the primary advantage their trading partners have in winning international projects. In project competitions, foreign governments assist their companies to structure the financing at a very early stage, thus providing a commitment and certainty to the customer, which is a powerful advantage that may sway the balance in their favor. Our own observations confirm that increasingly, financing is the focus of the competition.

Specifications: Foreign governments influence the project concept and design phase and steer the specifications or the pre-qualification criteria to best fit their exporters' skills and technologies, often before U.S. companies are even aware of a project. Many times, foreign governments get to host country decision-makers first, either actively generating opportunities for their exporters or cultivating relationships with procurement officials to "cherry pick" the best prospects for their respective companies.

---

opportunities and, where appropriate, influence the development of those opportunities—consistent with U.S. industry consensus; (2) to demonstrate U.S. Government financing support for proposals up front; and (3) to assist companies in enhancing their proposals. Significant interagency cooperation is required for early project development to work. Agencies target their combined efforts on priority projects in select markets.

Progress to Date

On behalf of competitive U.S. exporters, agencies have tried to target those pending and future projects where government efforts will make the greatest difference. With this approach in mind, Ex-Im Bank took the lead in developing more proactive trade financing options in Mexico, Brazil, and Russia in close cooperation with the Commerce Department and the U.S. Trade and Development Agency (USTDA).

Mexico: In Mexico, Ex-Im Bank focused on environmental municipal infrastructure opportunities and partnered with Mexican development bank BANOBRAS to host a conference in Mexico City in September 2002. The event attracted numerous Mexican cities and states and many U.S. exporters. A total of 37 projects were identified for U.S. exporters. Subsequently, funding from the Mexican Government has been slow. Ex-Im Bank and the development bank of Mexico (NAFIN) are currently working on a project that is designed to fund a number of these infrastructure projects.

USTDA continues to dedicate much of its activities in Mexico to the advancement of transportation infrastructure. Over the past few years, USTDA has financed feasibility studies for the modernization and expansion of the Puebla and Ciudad Obregón airports, the maritime port of Veracruz, and other studies dedicated to road and rail infrastructure. For example, a recent USTDA investment of $240,000 has generated over $150 million in U.S. exports related to the development and design of intermodal facilities in Mexico.

Brazil: Ex-Im Bank has developed a close working relationship with the Commercial Service in Brazil in pursuing potential projects. In November 2003, Ex-Im Bank, led by its Vice Chair, undertook a mission to Brazil. Mission participants, which included staff of the Commercial Service in Brazil, met with the Ministry of Planning and Budget to identify priority infrastructure projects under Brazil's planned $66 billion Public-Private Partnership. Ex-Im Bank has also developed strong working partnerships with major Brazilian banks, including Banco do Brasil, Banco Itau, Banco Unibanco, as well as with major Brazilian companies that include Petrobras, Companhia Vale do Rio Doce, and Odebrecht.

Seeing a tremendous opportunity in Brazil both for needed local development and for U.S. exports, USTDA has focused on opportunities related to the estimated $300 million per year that Brazilian railroads are investing to upgrade their infrastructure and rolling stock. USTDA provided a technical assistance grant to the Brazilian rail concessionaires to help improve logistics and safety and integrate their operations. In addition, USTDA funded an orientation visit, with the participation of the Commercial Service and Ex-Im

Bank, which helped highlight these business opportunities to U.S. rail companies. Working in partnership with the Commercial Service in Brazil, USTDA focused its project identification activities in FY 2003 on Petrobras refinery fire control projects, urban transport, and transportation security projects in the country.

Russia: In the Russian Federation, Ex-Im Bank has worked closely with USTDA in identifying potential projects, and has relied upon the Commerce Department's in-country presence via Commercial Service officers and representatives of BISNIS to develop these projects. For example, in the transportation sector USTDA has financed several feasibility studies, including a $350,000 grant for the reconstruction and modernization of Vnukovo Airport near Moscow. BISNIS representatives in St. Petersburg and Yekaterinburg established contacts with local companies that were interested in purchasing U.S. goods and services but were unaware of the financing options available. These efforts resulted in recent authorizations by Ex-Im Bank establishing a new credit for a medium-sized regional bank in Yekaterinburg and utilizing a portion of a pre-existing credit line for DeltaLeasing. Since a November 2003 meeting between the Chairman of Ex-Im Bank and the Russian Minister of Transportation, Commercial Service officers in Moscow have been working with Ministry officials to identify infrastructure and transportation security projects, and will assist with a proposed trade mission to the United States in spring 2004.

Finance and Advocacy

The TPCC agencies are ready to take early project development to the next level. The early project development concept pools the export promotion, trade finance, and advocacy efforts of the U.S. Government as a means of offsetting the financial and political support that foreign companies receive from their host governments. Leveraging the coordinated interest of the U.S. Government on behalf of U.S. companies will not only level the playing field but will also demonstrate the government's keen interest in seeing these projects through to fruition. In order for early project development to be fully realized, U.S. Government efforts must be combined with those of the exporting community early in the process.

Regular and formalized interagency coordination on priority projects is at the center of this approach. Ex-Im Bank and the Advocacy Center have signed a memorandum of understanding (MOU) that provides Advocacy Center clients an automatic referral process and expedited review for securing a letter of interest (LI)[1] from Ex-Im Bank at an early stage of the procurement process. This financing tool can be front-loaded into a company's proposal. An early LI often makes U.S. bids more enticing to foreign buyers, evaluating the relative merits by providing an early indication of financing interest at the beginning of the tender process. Since implementation of the MOU in February 2003,

---

1. Before a contract has been awarded, Ex-Im Bank assists exporters by providing an indication that financing may be available to creditworthy international buyers, both private and public sector, for purchases of U.S. goods and services. With Ex-Im Bank's loan guarantee, international buyers may be able to obtain competitive term financing from lenders when financing is not otherwise available.

the Advocacy Center has worked with Ex-Im Bank on $3 billion worth of LIs, which have already resulted in $600 million in deals.

In consultation with the TPCC and the Commercial Service, the Advocacy Center has taken the lead in advancing the early project development initiative within the Commerce Department. Once the Advocacy Center joins the Commercial Service as part of ITA's reorganization, new synergies will be created between Commercial Service posts and the finance agencies. The Advocacy Center will work directly with the posts and multilateral banks to identify projects and serve as the focal point for obtaining LIs. The Advocacy Center will fall under and assume the Commercial Service's MOU with OPIC, paving the way to support further joint efforts on behalf of U.S. investment in emerging markets.

The Advocacy Center plans to seek cooperative efforts with multilateral development banks as well. Coupling U.S. Government financing support with U.S. Government advocacy reinforces and augments the message communicated on behalf of U.S. exporters to foreign decision-makers.

Next Steps

There are several other steps TPCC agencies will take to provide a framework for implementing the early project development initiative. These include the following:

- Move the Advocacy Center to the Commercial Service. This will create new synergies between the Commercial Service posts and the finance agencies. The Advocacy Center will work directly with these posts to identify projects before they go out to bid and will serve as the focal point for obtaining LIs.

- Market Ex-Im Bank's LI to Commercial Service posts and make posts fully aware that this tool is available. Ex-Im Bank and the Commercial Service will work together to increase awareness of the LI's availability and establish efficient operating procedures for its use by Commercial Service posts.

Success Story: Case Study in Early Advocacy and Financing

Landrum & Brown (L&B), a small Ohio architectural firm, came to the Commerce Department's Advocacy Center for support on a bid for the expansion design of the Beijing Capital International Airport for the 2008 Olympics. Advocacy Center staff assisted L&B in filing a letter of interest (LI) application, which was submitted to Ex-Im Bank for expedited review under the memorandum of understanding (MOU). Ex-Im Bank issued the LI to the company, which L&B included in tender documents submitted to the Chinese Government. In further support of L&B's bid, USTDA offered a $350,000 training grant contingent upon L&B winning the tender. The Advocacy Center coordinated advocacy letters from Commerce Secretary Donald Evans, Transportation Secretary Norman Mineta, and Ohio Governor Bob Taft—all of which emphasized the significant U.S. Government financing support demonstrated in L&B's proposal.

Although L&B was the runner-up in the competition (receiving $500,000 compensation for its presentation), the company believes U.S. Government support improved its business prospects in China, where dozens of airport expansions are planned over the next few years. In fact, L&B has recently been short-listed on the competition for the redesign of the Shanghai airport. The Advocacy Center has organized the same coordinated support (including an Ex-Im Bank LI and a USTDA training grant) provided on the Beijing tender. A decision on the project is expected soon.

Developing Multilateral Development Bank Opportunities

Projects financed by multilateral development banks (MDBs) represent multi-billion dollar commercial opportunities for U.S. companies. As global competition for these projects increases, the United States must remain innovative and proactive in its efforts to ensure that our companies are able to compete effectively.

A new pilot project, to be implemented by the Commercial Service in cooperation with other TPCC agencies, meets this need by tailoring the early project development concept and goals to give U.S. companies an early advantage in competing for "demand-driven" World Bank-funded opportunities. By targeting this particular subset of World Bank projects, where regional and local governments in the client country drive the demand for products and services to be procured, U.S. companies can take advantage of a window of opportunity to showcase their products as needs are assessed and procurement plans are drawn up, not after tenders are already issued. As an initial step, the pilot program is targeting projects worth over $1.5 billion in some of the major growth markets identified by the TPCC, such as China, Russia, and Mexico. Projects being pursued include opportunities in health, irrigation, and environmental technologies. The success of the program will be evaluated on an ongoing basis, with an eye toward expanding the number of projects and markets that are targeted. This initiative will build on ongoing USTDA multilateral development bank trust fund activities that support early project development.

- Improve the information flow between the Commercial Service, USTDA, and Ex-Im Bank. These agencies will support the Advocacy Center's work with the posts in identifying priority projects in key markets and fully utilizing Ex-Im Banks' LIs. Ex-Im Bank will develop web-based information to increase posts' familiarity with Ex-Im Bank programs.

- Early project development trade missions, perhaps with rotating U.S. Government team leaders drawn from Ex-Im Bank, OPIC, USTDA, State Economic Bureau, and the Commerce Department, along with private sector firms will be considered.

- Focus on World Bank-funded opportunities in key foreign markets. Working with the Commercial Service, TPCC agencies will select projects in which local interest in U.S. products, services, and technology can be fostered before tenders are announced and bids are made.

- Continue outreach to U.S. companies, associations, and industry trade groups to inform them of this new approach and to gather additional information to continuously improve client support.

Mixed Credits

A major concern of the U.S. exporting community reported in the 2002 National Export Strategy is the effectiveness with which our major trading partners use tied aid financing to promote exports to developing countries. As expected, U.S. exporters want the U.S. Government to continue to aggressively police foreign tied aid use and to actively counter any remaining instances of trade-distorting tied aid that is in violation of the letter or the spirit of rules of the Organization for Economic Cooperation and Development. However, they also want the U.S. Government to use tied aid proactively to fund development-related capital projects the way that many foreign governments do.

In an effort to address this issue while focusing on the Administration's developmental agenda, the TPCC agencies devised a new process for combining Agency for

International Development (USAID) grants with Ex-Im Bank standard financing. This approach is designed to allow select developing nations assume part of the cost of development projects while still benefiting from development assistance grants. The goal is to provide creditworthy host countries with the flexibility to support more projects with fewer developmental dollars, while increasing the potential participation of U.S. exporters.

A project must satisfy certain conditions. It must be commercially non-viable—that is, the project's cash flow cannot service market-based or standard ECA financing over ten years (normally); it must fit within the USAID development strategy and budgetary constraints for the country; and it must be eligible for at least medium-term public-sector support from Ex-Im Bank. There are about $4 billion worth of projects won annually by our foreign competitors using similar aid financing mechanisms of their governments.

Pilot Project

USAID and Ex-Im Bank have worked over the past year to communicate the availability of mixed credits to USAID missions, develop procedures for structuring and implementing a mixed credit, and identify potential mixed credit projects. Given the sometimes difficult nature of assembling a transaction under a new financing mechanism, agencies have agreed to focus on one particularly promising project in the near term. The first project will be a rural electrification project in Guatemala that involves a 4.5-megawatt wind-generated power plant with a diesel backup. A developer has been identified.

Once the TPCC agencies have had practical experience with using a mixed credit approach on this project, they will evaluate the success of the tool, the potential scope of its future application, and whether the process of using it can be facilitated.

Joint Marketing

During our interviews with exporters leading up to the 2002 National Export Strategy, companies reported that they were confused about how the agencies worked together. From their perspective, the agencies were one entity—"the government"—and they expected the various programs to fully leverage each other.

Based in part on this input—but also on the need to reach out to more companies—the TPCC launched an interagency marketing group in 2002. This group developed an integrated strategy to reach existing and potential exporters. The effort included direct mail, joint participation in major trade shows, exporter symposia, and other activities to educate exporters about opportunities and resources available through TPCC agencies.

Joint Mailing and Seminars

The joint mailing campaign that began in 2003 has continued. The Commerce Department, SBA, and OPIC collaborate with Ex-Im Bank in distributing an electronic newsletter to 85,000 U.S. exporters. The newsletter contains articles on all the TPCC agencies' programs. The Commerce Department also includes articles on SBA, Ex-Im Bank, USTDA, OPIC, and Agriculture Department programs in its Export America publication. In fall 2003, the TPCC agencies conducted a direct mail campaign that brought in 173 qualified leads. Ex-Im Bank, working through the Commerce Department's domestic offices, conducted 36 seminars around the country—up from 33 in 2002.

Before: The U.S. Export Assistance Pavilion before TPCC agencies developed a unified pavilion.

After: The unified pavilion at the 2004 National Association of Manufacturers' trade show in Chicago, February 2004.

Trade Shows

In 2002 the TPCC agencies created an export assistance pavilion in order to show their programs and services in one spot at major trade shows. The trade show organizers liked the concept, and the agencies have attended five shows. In 2004, with input from the major trade show operators, the TPCC agencies have pooled their money and purchased a modular exhibit that gives them a unified and more organized look. This has proven to be a major success, with numerous trade shows now asking the agencies to bring the exhibit to their shows, offering free prime space. This in turn has led to an increase in the number of sales leads garnered by the participants. At the recent National Association of Manufacturers Show in February 2004, for example, agencies had more than 600 inquiries, and 100 companies spoke with TPCC agency representatives and trade specialists. The first three shows where the pavilion has appeared have averaged 200 prospects per show.

Interagency Training

One of the most often mentioned suggestions that exporters had in meetings with them three years ago was that government officials take a more coordinated approach in their delivery of services to the public. As one focus group participant phrased it, "We need someone to help us through the maze." Subsequent studies have confirmed that exporters and would-be exporters would greatly benefit from having the agencies be better informed about one another's programs and be better able to guide companies through the export process by making accurate referrals and providing useful follow-up throughout the process.

TPCC Interagency Trade Officer Training Program

Based on feedback from the business community, the TPCC designed the Interagency Trade Officer Training Program to train experienced international trade officers on the full range of export promotion programs and services offered by the TPCC member agencies. More important, the program focuses on real-world application of these programs to drive successful export marketing campaigns for American companies, especially SMEs. The objective is to prepare the next generation of international trade officers to accurately and holistically gauge their customers' real needs and export objectives and to seamlessly package and deliver an effective, customized solution that integrates a multitude of services from the TPCC agencies. By broadening the perspective and skills of our staff who deliver trade promotion programs and services, the Federal Government can provide service to the customer that goes beyond a mere export sale—taking U.S. companies from one transaction, to several new markets, and even to investment abroad where appropriate.

2003 Pilot Phase: The agenda developed by the TPCC emphasizes account management skills and an overview of federal resources and programs. Participants become knowledgeable of the full range of U.S. Government tools available to U.S. companies wanting to do business abroad.

In 2003, the TPCC completed three pilot sessions of the Interagency Trade Officer Training course. During this pilot phase, the TPCC trained 92 staff from 10 federal agencies and two states. This was very much of a team effort, with the Departments of Commerce and Agriculture, OPIC, and Ex-Im Bank contributing to the funding, USTDA providing the training facility, and other participating agencies sending staff both as trainers and participants to the course. Each session has built on the last, incorporating the comments and suggestions of participants to improve the course and sharpen its focus.

Reaction to the course has been very positive, with most of the participants indicating they greatly value the face-to-face interaction with colleagues from other agencies. Participants have said that they have used the contacts developed during the training to expand and improve service to their clients. Even the most experienced participants have said they sharpened their skills and made valuable contacts in other agencies that will help them improve the quality of service they provide to U.S. firms.

Next Steps: An interagency training task force is working to organize three more sessions in 2004 and to turn the pilot program into a more permanent offering. Five agencies (the Departments of Commerce and Agriculture, SBA, Ex-Im Bank, and OPIC) have committed funds, and USTDA has again contributed the use of its conference facility. These agencies formalized their cooperation and the pooling of resources with an interagency MOU and together selected a contractor to help organize the sessions and further develop the program.

A significant challenge for the TPCC will be how to reach greater numbers of trade officers throughout the United States and the world. Technological solutions (such as distance learning via the Internet) do exist, but cannot replace the valuable interaction that occurs among participants in the current format. The goal will be to find new ways to expand the program and leverage resources without eliminating the person-to-person knowledge exchange and networking between trade officers that the TPCC encourages.

State Department Commercial Training

The State Department's Foreign Service Institute (FSI) continues to expand its training offerings in the areas of trade development, promotion, and compliance. Its courses are open to all government agencies. In 2002, FSI launched a new course on trade agreement monitoring and implementation. In 2003, there were four offerings at FSI and one in Beijing, training a total of 140 officers. Additional sessions are scheduled for 2004.

FSI is now developing an online distance-learning course designed for Foreign Service officers and Foreign Service national employees already in the field. Initial case studies focus on compliance with World Trade Organization rules and protection of intellectual property rights. Other modules will be developed as funding becomes available.

The Foreign Service Institute also offers a Commercial Tradecraft course to enhance staff expertise in advocating for and assisting U.S. businesses, protecting intellectual property rights, and helping companies take full advantage of the programs of OPIC and Ex-Im Bank. More specialized courses, including those on energy issues, telecommunications, aviation, biotechnology, and dispute resolution are also offered on a regular basis.

Services

Services have played an increasingly important role in the U.S. economy, U.S. employment, and U.S. exports. In 2002, services accounted for three-quarters of private sector GDP and for nearly four-fifths of private non-farm employment—86 million jobs in all. The United States exported $279 billion in commercial services in 2002—29 percent of the U.S. goods and services export total—for a services trade surplus of $74 billion. The United States ranks as the world's premier services exporter, with U.S. services exports accounting for 17 percent of the $1.5 trillion global services exports total in 2002. U.S. exporters need the Federal Government to develop trade and finance tools uniquely suited to this highly specialized part of the economy. The TPCC agencies have been active in several key sectors.

Technology Industry

Ex-Im Bank's Technology Industry Initiative:
While Ex-Im Bank has been providing support for this sector—typically in conjunction with exports of capital goods—it is now providing more focused and targeted support. As a first step, Ex-Im Bank has formed a Technology Committee that brings together a senior level group to concentrate on opportunities to assist the high technology industry with their exports. The committee's focus will be to meet with industry participants and to obtain a first-hand understanding of the industry's unique characteristics and dynamics and of the competitive environment and challenges that confront the industry in the international arena. Ex-Im Bank's objective is to identify what it can do to help these companies compete more effectively by developing new or modified credit insurance and loan guarantee products or by considering other new approaches to policy or procedures in order to broaden credit support. Ex-Im Bank expects this committee to spearhead its efforts to meet the evolving needs of this important and growing segment of the U.S. exporting community.

Financial Services

USTDA is working with USAID and other public and private entities to advance the export of U.S. financial services to certain countries. This is being undertaken in order to train those countries to do bond financing and to develop other new financial mechanisms for important infrastructure needs. USTDA is funding technical assistance activities in this sector to advance projects in India, Vietnam, China, and Turkey.

Travel and Tourism

The 2002 National Export Strategy highlights the U.S. travel and tourism industry as a sector that faces significant foreign competition and that was particularly hard hit in the aftermath of September 11, 2001. TPCC agencies have responded with initiatives that improve federal services through better coordination among agencies and with the private sector.

Services Initiative of the Commercial Service

The Commercial Service continues to improve its support of U.S. SME clients that export services. The Services Initiative launched in 2000 resulted in four cross-disciplinary industry sector teams, new market research, and training opportunities for our trade professionals. The Commercial Service is building upon this success by identifying export promotion products and services that meet the needs of services sector clients, as well as expanding training opportunities for staff. The result will be an increase in the number and type of services sector clients that succeed abroad.

U.S. travel and tourism promotion campaign: In 2004, the Commerce Department will launch a $6 million international marketing campaign in the United Kingdom designed to expand the volume and export value of British travelers to the United States. The campaign represents the first time funding has been made available for an integrated marketing effort to promote the United States as a premier destination of choice. The United Kingdom represents the top overseas market for the United States and is heavily marketed by key competitors, causing U.S. loss of market share from this key travel segment. The campaign will incorporate media (TV) advertising, cooperative marketing programs with industry, and public relations events and sponsorships.

More available Commerce Department travel and tourism data: Within the Commerce Department, the Office of Travel and Tourism Industries (OTTI) and the Bureau of Economic Analysis (BEA) have an ongoing MOU to improve the availability of international travel data critical to the sector. Supported by OTTI, BEA has developed the Travel and Tourism Satellite Accounts (TTSA) that rearrange data from the national economic accounts and other sources for the purpose of more completely analyzing specific economic activity. Because tourism data are not separately identified in the national accounts, the TTSA are particularly useful for assessing the effects of the September 11 attacks. BEA has released quarterly estimates of total travel and tourism sales since 2002. Based on OTTI monthly and quarterly data, BEA also develops estimates for travel and passenger fair imports and exports. It also provides total travel spending estimates for over 30 countries and several regional breakouts. Data coming out of this cooperation are available on both BEA's and OTTI's Web sites.

Travel and Tourism Team training: The Travel and Tourism Team (a cross-disciplinary industry sector team of the Commercial Service) has been working to improve cooperation among federal agencies related to tourism and to improve the products and services offered to the industry. There are about 80 members of the team, which is comprised of several OTTI staff and Commercial Service staff from the domestic and foreign field. In 2003, the Team held a training session in conjunction with the Travel Industry Association's Marketing Outlook Forum that was attended by over 30 team members. Topics included how the Team could better utilize the research data issued by OTTI and how multiple public and private tourism entities could best access the international travel market. As a result of this training, OTTI initiated a dialogue between the Team and USDA's Rural Tourism group.

The Tourism Policy Council: The Tourism Policy Council (TPC) and Tourism Policy Council Working Group (consisting of 15 federal agencies and offices) met several times in 2003 to discuss cooperative efforts to assist the travel and tourism industries. The group developed a TPC Alerts communication system to keep the federal agencies, travel associations, and other key contacts informed of the new U.S. entry/exit system, changes in U.S. visa policy, and other issues related to facilitating travel to the United States. The group received updates on the latest international travel data and developed possible opportunities for cooperative marketing efforts among the federal partners.

U.S./Japan Tourism Export Expansion Initiative: The Commerce Department has a formal MOU with the Japanese Ministry of Land, Infrastructure, and Transport to conduct a tourism promotion initiative between the two countries in order to foster mutual economic growth and improved cultural exchange. The tangible goal set forth in the initiative was to expand the travel and tourism traveler base over a five-year span (through 2006) between the United States and Japan, to a level approaching that in 2000. The OTTI is working with the Commercial Service in Tokyo on this effort.

The MOU established the Tourism Export Expansion Council. Industry leaders representing a cross section of the tourism sector lead the initiative. Successes of the initiative include increased acceptance of U.S. debit and credit cards by Japanese vendors, steps to translate Japanese driver's licenses for rental car use in the United States, and familiarization tours and publicity campaigns to attract travel to both countries.

State Department air services initiatives: The State Department—supported by the Departments of Transportation and Commerce—leads negotiations for air services agreements, which reap benefits for travelers, exporters, and airport communities and make cargo transport more efficient. In addition to the more than 60 Open Skies agreements in place globally with countries of all economic profiles, State is working to conclude a comprehensive air services agreement with the European Union to significantly open the transatlantic aviation market. The U.S. Government is also expanding air rights in Asia (for example, Hong Kong, Vietnam, Thailand, China) and is seeking greater access to Russian, Middle Eastern, and South Asian markets.

Transportation Security

The international transportation system is critical to the U.S. economy. As noted in the 2003 National Export Strategy Report, economies must promote the efficient and reliable movement of people and goods across borders, without allowing transportation systems to become tools of terrorism. This new challenge has made the U.S. transportation security and safety industry a key growth sector, and has required closer coordination among agencies.

USTDA transportation security and safety: USTDA's traditional program relies heavily upon U.S. service providers and promotes exports of both services and goods. The agency's recent Transportation Security and Safety Initiative, which was developed in cooperation with U.S. service providers, has a heavy emphasis on the export of U.S. services, since American companies are on the cutting edge of technology and expertise in these areas. This initiative serves as a premiere opportunity for U.S. service providers with expertise in cost-benefit analysis, transportation management, information and communication technology, project management, and supply-chain security and logistics to export their services.

Data Management Improvement Act (DMIA) Task Force: The Task Force was established under the auspices of the DMIA, enacted in 2000. It is a program of the U.S. Department of Homeland Security's Border and Transportation Security Directorate. U.S. Government agencies that contribute to this effort are the Departments of Homeland Security, State, Commerce, and Transportation. There are 12 private sector travel and tourism associations that also serve on the Task Force. Numerous site visits were conducted to view land, air, and sea points of entry to determine what would be needed to improve the system. The focus this year was on (1) port-of-entry facility and infrastructure issues; (2) facilitation of traffic flow; (3) identification and enhancement of cooperation and coordination mechanisms among the public and private sectors, as well as among state, federal, and local agencies and the affected foreign governments; (4) analysis of a variety of information technology systems; and (5) development of a conceptual border management system. As a result of the meetings and visits, the group developed and issued its second report to Congress on this effort.

State and Local Outreach

As highlighted in the 2002 and 2003 National Export Strategies, collaboration between federal trade agencies and state trade organizations is critical because companies frequently look to their states for help in penetrating foreign markets. For this reason, the TPCC agencies have developed solid relationships with the states over the years.

Through the U.S. Export Assistance Centers (USEACs), federal and state agencies cooperate on a wide range of activities. In 18 states, the USEAC offices are physically co-located with state export promotion offices. The USEACs support the states' foreign trade missions, and are now jointly sponsoring and promoting trade missions with many states. The USEACs work closely with the states on seminars and conferences to raise awareness of business opportunities. Some USEACs also publish newsletters in conjunction with their state partners and work closely with state travel and tourism offices to draw foreign visitors.

New Models for Federal-State Cooperation

The TPCC agencies are now working to establish more sophisticated partnerships with state export promotion agencies. All parties are finding that they must leverage each other's resources to provide the trade promotion services businesses need. The 2003 National Export Strategy highlighted partnerships in New Jersey, Michigan, and Florida. States that have curtailed their international offices, such as Connecticut and New Mexico, are ensuring that their businesses have access to trade promotion services by funding qualified firms to take advantage of federal programs. The Department of Agriculture is an experienced leader in this area, and has been active in educating other TPCC members. Cooperation can include packages of federal services, joint strategic planning sessions to coordinate trade events, and joint training and outreach efforts.

The TPCC agencies are now attempting to use federal services to strategically target exporting and investment opportunities for firms from a particular state.

Hawaii: The Platinum Key Service agreement between the State of Hawaii and the Commercial Service targets China. The agreement provides specific project information and business development assistance to Hawaii energy, engineering, environmental, and planning firms interested in work on the estimated $20 billion worth of infrastructure projects planned by Beijing to prepare the city to host the 2008 Summer Olympics. Currently, Hawaii is the only state with such an agreement.

California: In California, where the Commerce and Agriculture Departments and SBA have been active, the TPCC agencies are working toward new models of collaboration in areas such as training and trade financing. With the elimination of the California Trade and Commerce Agency, many of the stakeholders have begun discussions aimed at ensuring that California firms still have access to needed services through a partnership between the State of California and those Federal Government agencies involved with international trade.

The Commercial Service, along with key units within the Commerce Department's International Trade Administration, will work to expand its partnership-building in California. This will involve, through the TPCC, other key federal agencies and programs to be determined as the partnership develops. This proposal will leverage our existing resources within the state, including strong infrastructure and cooperative agreements that currently exist between TPCC members to provide services to California firms in a coordinated, collaborative fashion. The Commercial Service proposes to work in close consultation with the state to make sure that key industries identified by the state benefit from participation in selected trade events both locally and overseas.

Success Story: Rockford, Illinois, Area Firm Lands Export Contracts to Mexico

Metz Tool and Die Works, Inc., like many industrial businesses in the Rockford, Illinois, area, was experiencing hard times due to a decline in sales. Don Metz, the owner, felt the major reason for the lost sales was low-quality, low-priced imports and decided to seek help from his congressional representative. Congressman Manzullo introduced him to the Chicago U.S. Export Assistance Center (USEAC) to find new export markets. The Commerce Department and the U.S. Agency for International Development worked with Mr. Metz to identify strong potential markets for his product and prepare him for a successful transition into foreign trade. Among other activities, Mr. Metz joined a trade mission to Mexico led by SBA.

Following this initial introduction to potential buyers, Mr. Metz received several requests for bids on specific projects. He provided specifications, samples, and final bids with his standard terms (essentially, cash in advance or substantial progress payments prior to delivery). After several such bids were declined, Mr. Metz was finally given a frank explanation: Even though his higher price was more than offset by the superior quality of his product, would-be buyers were unable to meet his payment terms.

Mr. Metz returned to the USEAC staff for help with financing. SBA provided a guarantee for a $500,000 Export Working Capital Loan from AMCORE Bank so that the company could build and ship the product without need of prepayment from the buyer. Ex-Im Bank provided a credit insurance policy so that the company could grant the buyer 60 days following delivery for payment.

By adding competitive financing terms to his next bid, Mr. Metz received a firm order for a $150,000 mold and eventually reaped more than $1,000,000 in sales during his first year as an exporter.

The partnership envisions using currently existing public and private sector organizations within the state to promote businesses in California and to expand overseas export opportunities for SMEs that create jobs in California. This model uses the 15 USEACs in California, the Centers for International Trade Development (CITDs), local chambers of commerce, trade associations, and world trade centers to identify and then assist export-ready California firms.

Under this model, the State of California and the Commercial Service would enter into a public-private partnership with the existing trade service providers located in every major city in California. The partnership will include a formal program of training of the service providers and ongoing technical support through Web-based and electronic services of the federal agencies. The coordination, prioritization, and agreed-upon division of responsibilities of these organizations would be formulated through a California trade promotion strategy developed under state leadership. Key elements of the partnership include overseas support, joint training, and trade finance solutions.

Overseas Support: To directly assist California exporters in overseas markets, the Commercial Service and Foreign Agricultural Service offices overseas may deliver a range of free and fee-based targeted services to the state.

The Commercial Service is offering its new Platinum Key Service—a customized bundle of fee-based services designed to support the state's trade objectives in a specific market. The State and the Commercial Service have agreed to begin piloting the Platinum Key Service in California, with a view toward entering into a broader, formal agreement with the Commercial Service when California's trade promotion authority is restored. The Commercial Service in Spain will serve as the target market for 90 days. During this time, the Commercial Service will work with the State, key California trade promotion organizations, USEAC partner agencies, and exporters to deliver the variety of services available under the Platinum Key Service Program.

The free services of the Commercial Service and the Foreign Agricultural Service can be provided from any of these agencies' overseas offices, while the Platinum Key Service program may be used in key markets that the state selects.

The range of free and fee-based services could include:

- Addressing basic market inquiries and providing assistance with trade complaints

- Providing market intelligence and highlighting trade opportunities in key California sectors

- Conducting customized market research for the state or for individual firms

- Identifying qualified local partners and distributors for California exporters

- Organizing highly sophisticated trade promotion events, including California trade and investment missions or company-specific events

- Providing advocacy and tracking for California firms on major projects

- Organizing California State pavilions in key trade shows

Costs of this type of partnership would be a fraction of the costs of establishing the state's own offices overseas, but partnership members could still work with any future state regional offices overseas or directly with California-based offices and partners.

Joint Training: The proposed training program is modeled after the TPCC Interagency Trade Officer Training Program developed at the Federal Government level. The training program was designed in response to research that showed most SMEs are not aware of the wide range of federal resources available to help them do business internationally. Furthermore, although firms that use federal services are fairly happy with the support, a majority of firms complain that the services of the various agencies are not well coordinated and that they need guidance to help them find and use the right services. The training is aimed at the core trade facilitation service providers in California. These include managers from the CITDs, USEACs, selected world trade centers, local economic development corporations, the California Department of Food and Agriculture, and other providers of trade services.

Trade Finance Solutions: Ex-Im Bank and SBA will begin working with a designated state agency to identify ways to provide export finance or insurance support for California exporters. More detail on this will be available once the state designates an agency or official to begin discussions.

Dedicated Resource: The Commercial Service has assigned a senior Foreign Service officer to an existing Commercial Service position in Sacramento to oversee all aspects of this program, outside the services already covered under the joint Agriculture Team of the Departments of Agriculture and Commerce. Once the program is under way, that officer will coordinate the delivery of the programs and services with and to the state. Responsibilities would include working with the statewide service providers, assessing needs and capabilities, establishing market and service priorities, and coordinating services with the overseas and Washington-based partners.

The state's role will be to provide a central point for developing and coordinating California's trade promotion strategy. State leadership would also provide a branding of California as a trade, tourism, and investment power and would allow service providers to promote the California brand under a statewide program.

The California model is designed to help the state and California business community leverage existing resources so that California companies have the support they need to successfully enter global markets. At the same time, these programs are intended to serve as a model that can be replicated, as a whole or in part, by other states that need to augment and/or replace their existing trade promotion programs.

An Export Promotion Strategy for China

Since 2000, no foreign market has received more attention than China. The initial focus was China's accession to the World Trade Organization (WTO). Now the objective is to ensure that China's implementation of its WTO commitments is carried out in full and to take advantage of expanding market opportunities. While U.S. exports to China have increased 75 percent since 2000, U.S. companies are concerned that they are not exporting as much as they would expect in a number of sectors. They highlight that while the U.S. share of world exports is 11 percent, their share of China's import market is only 8 percent (Chart 4).

This Administration is committed to providing U.S. exporters with the right tools and a level playing field in the global marketplace. Where Chinese competitors rely on inappropriate, unfair, or market-distorting practices, the U.S. Government will respond aggressively through U.S. trade laws, compliance efforts, and multilateral negotiations.

This year, in line with WTO commitments, Chinese tariffs will continue to decrease, some to their lowest levels, and additional non-tariff barriers will be eliminated. As a result, wholly foreign-owned enterprises will be able to freely import and export most products into and out of China; wholly foreign-owned enterprises may be established to engage in commissioned agent, wholesaling, and retail businesses (with some exceptions); and the direct selling sector will be re-opened. For these reasons, the TPCC agencies are renewing their focus on expanding export opportunities for U.S. businesses in China's market.

In December 2003, President Bush and Premier Wen agreed that significantly increasing U.S. exports to China would be a priority of both governments and that the U.S.-China Joint Commission on Commerce and Trade (JCCT) would be a key vehicle for accomplishing that goal. U.S. Commerce Secretary Evans, U.S. Trade Representative Zoellick, and Chinese Vice

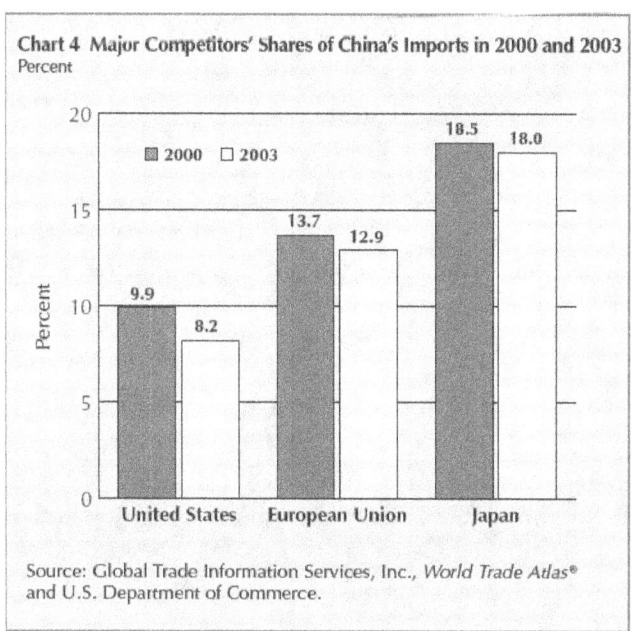

Chart 4 Major Competitors' Shares of China's Imports in 2000 and 2003
Percent

Source: Global Trade Information Services, Inc., *World Trade Atlas®* and U.S. Department of Commerce.

23

Premier Wu are scheduled to chair the next meeting of the JCCT in spring 2004 in Washington, D.C., during which the United States and China hope to agree to a strategy to increase opportunities for U.S. exports to China. Key elements of this strategy will be (1) raising awareness among U.S. exporters of the opportunities in China, including identification of sectors that will enjoy the most new access and benefit the most from lower tariffs, and (2) working with the Chinese Government to lower the cost for potential U.S. exporters of travel to China by offering lower cost services to small business exporters from the United States (China Council for Promotion of International Trade [CCPIT] and New England states). High-level visits will also be a central component of this strategy, including the trip to the United States by Vice Premier Wu and a trip to China by Commerce Department Secretary Evans coinciding with a trip by representatives of the President's Export Council. The U.S. Government will support a trade mission by the National Association of Manufacturers later in the year to explore improved opportunities for exporting U.S. manufactured goods.

Priority Sectors

The Commerce Department and the U.S. Trade and Development Agency (USTDA) have identified a set of priority sectors that represent the best opportunities for U.S. exports:

- Transportation (including aviation, air traffic control, and airports)

- Energy

- Healthcare (medical equipment and pharmaceuticals)

- Information technology

- Agriculture

These sectors will drive U.S. Government trade promotion activities, including trade missions and events, and ensure that future JCCT efforts are focused on sectors where U.S. companies are most competitive and the opportunities are greatest.

Activities and Programs

The Commerce Department's International Trade Administration (ITA) will continue to develop a list of activities and programs for 2004 that support U.S. export development in each of the priority sectors (for example, trade missions leading up to and following the JCCT meeting, and Platinum Key Service agreements for U.S. states focused on China).

Work to date in key sectors includes:

Transportation: The Commerce Department, in conjunction with the U.S.-China Business Council and the U.S. Coalition of Service Industries, is working with China's National Development and Reform Commission to organize a logistics conference in spring 2004 to show Chinese policymakers the benefits of minimal direct government intervention in the logistics sector. The Commerce Department's ultimate goal in this effort is that China will develop an environment where highly efficient logistics systems can be fostered, to the benefit of U.S. companies' products in China and for U.S. logistics companies.

Healthcare: The Commerce Department and the Department of Health and Human Services are working with several Chinese ministries and U.S. industry representatives to conduct a Healthcare Forum in May 2004. The forum should help U.S. and Chinese officials improve healthcare delivery throughout China and provide U.S. companies greater access to potential buyers.

In addition, the Commerce Department's Office of Microelectronics, Medical Equipment, and Instrumentation will lead a medical device trade mission to Beijing and Chengdu in April 2004. This trade mission will be held as a work plan activity of the JCCT's Medical Devices and Pharmaceuticals Subgroup. The Subgroup, which is co-chaired on the Chinese side by the State Food and Drug Administration, addresses medical device and pharmaceutical regulatory issues of concern to U.S. industry. U.S. participants in the April Subgroup include the Commerce Department, the U.S. Food and Drug Administration, and the Department of Justice, as well as U.S. industry associations and American Chamber of Commerce in China representatives.

> ### USTDA Organizing Healthcare Sector Initiatives in Support of U.S. Industry
>
> USTDA has actively pursued projects in healthcare and related sectors where U.S. companies are competitive in the export of goods and services for project implementation. In support of these programs, USTDA has funded a number of reverse trade missions (orientation visits) for Chinese officials to visit U.S. companies that are able to supply emergency response communication systems. In addition, USTDA is positioned to support projects that will assist Chinese hospitals in receiving international accreditation, which will necessarily provide an opportunity for U.S. suppliers of high-tech medical equipment and devices to serve this new market. USTDA is also assessing opportunities to assist China in promulgating new standards for infectious disease control, thereby opening opportunities for U.S. exports in the upgrading of China's healthcare system.

Energy: The U.S. Departments of Commerce and Energy, along with USTDA, are continuing their participation in the Oil and Gas Forum, which the United States will co-host with a number of Chinese ministries. The forum will allow U.S. companies to showcase their capabilities as well as discuss with the Chinese ways of improving market access. The fifth meeting of the annual forum will be held in summer 2004 in China.

Information technology: The Commerce Department led a microelectronics trade mission to Semicon China in March 2004. The Commerce Department and China's Ministry of Information Industry are co-hosting the third China-American Telecommunications Summit in Chicago, and will also co-organize the third U.S.-China Informatization Policy Roundtable with China's State Council Informatization Office later this year. These forums provide U.S. information technology companies with access to key decision-makers responsible for regulating this sector in China.

Agriculture: In January 2004, USDA's Administrator of the Foreign Agricultural Service announced the opening of new Agricultural Trade Offices (ATOs) in Beijing and Manila. U.S. exports of agricultural products to China are forecast to reach $5.4 billion this fiscal year, compared with $3.5 billion sold in 2003 and $1.8 billion in 2002.

China is the fourth-largest export market for U.S. agricultural products and has recently become a strong market for U.S. soybeans. In addition to the new Beijing ATO, FAS operates ATOs in Shanghai and Guangzhou. The opening of a third ATO in China underscores the importance of this market to the U.S. agricultural industry.

Trade Missions

Trade missions will be a key feature of TPCC efforts in 2004, with missions occurring both prior to and after the JCCT Ministerial. Planned missions by sector include microelectronics, consumer goods, medical devices, fluid power equipment, machine tools, agricultural machinery, and plastics. In addition, a number of states will take trade missions to China, including Florida, Illinois, Nebraska, New Hampshire, New York, and Virginia. In order to ensure that these missions are successful, the U. S. Government is working with the Chinese Government to get its help to (1) ensure high-level participation at meetings, (2) donate meeting space as needed, and (3) include Chinese companies and state-owned enterprises interested in buying from U.S. companies that participate in the meetings.

Priority Projects

The Commerce Department is developing a list of priority projects that will be ready for signature in time for the JCCT Ministerial or the Secretarial trade mission. The Department will also identify strategic projects which, if won, would represent a significant market opening for other U.S. goods and services (e.g., by introducing a U.S. product standard in China). Prior to the JCCT Ministerial, a comprehensive advocacy strategy will be developed for each priority project (e.g., courtesy calls, letters or demarches, representational meetings and visits). Regular discussions will be held in China with the Ministry of Commerce (MOFCOM) on priority projects and on the matching of smaller U.S. companies with Chinese bid winners via a sub-supplier initiative.

As part of the JCCT efforts, the Commerce Department has asked the Chinese Government to finalize the Framework Agreement between the Ministry of Finance and the Export-Import Bank of the United States (Ex-Im Bank). While the absence of this agreement does not stop companies from using Ex-Im Bank, its implementation will help to streamline the export financing process for projects and transactions involving U.S. exports.

Small Business

The Commerce Department, the Small Business Administration (SBA), and Ex-Im Bank will work to implement a three-pronged strategy centered on (1) training Chinese ministry officials in how governments can help support small business development, (2) developing alliances between the U.S. and Chinese small business communities, and (3) identifying trade finance options for Chinese buyers. A number of possible steps are being considered, including:

- Exchanging small business delegations to share technical expertise and experience in small business development strategies.

- Establishing a training program to share information on products and services that facilitate small business exports.

- Bringing small groups of Chinese companies to the United States to buy U.S. products, with the Commercial Service assisting in the organization of meetings with U.S. companies.

- Linking the CCPIT and BuyUSA Web sites.

- Developing a Chinese program (All-China Federation of Industry and Commerce) to fund travel by U.S. SMEs on trade missions to China.

- Using the Commerce Department's International Buyer Program to bring Chinese buyers to U.S. trade shows (focusing on non-visa-related sectors).

- Offering meeting space to help defray costs of U.S. companies visiting China (to be carried out by MOFCOM).

- Creating an Ex-Im Bank facility with the China Development Bank (CDB) for Chinese small businesses that want to purchase goods and services from U.S. companies.

In September 2003, senior managers of Ex-Im Bank met with the CDB in Beijing to find common ground in their mandates to assist small- and medium-size enterprises (SMEs). During the meeting, it was proposed that Ex-Im Bank make a $100 million Credit Guarantee Facility available to the CDB. These funds would be used to on-lend to Chinese SMEs that import goods and services from the United States. Since CDB knows its market best and has the ability to conduct the credit analysis on Chinese companies, CDB would make the credit judgment and assume the risk on SME importers/end-users. Under this scenario, Ex-Im Bank would assume only the CDB risk.

Outreach

The Commerce Department's Manufacturing and Services, Market Access and Compliance, and Commercial Service units have developed a program designed to guide U.S. companies through the stages necessary for doing business in China, including important themes for SMEs. This program has already been presented to U.S. companies in five cities, and the Commerce Department has developed a list of other target cities in which it intends to market this program. The Commerce Department will continue to improve the content of the program through the incorporation of a visiting U.S. Commercial Service officer from China.

Conclusion

China is an important market for the United States, given its potential size, the success that U.S. small businesses have exporting to China (30 percent of U.S. exports to China are by small businesses), and improved market access due to reduced tariff and non-tariff barriers resulting from China's WTO accession. For these reasons, the TPCC agencies have made it a priority for the Federal Government to have a coherent and serious trade promotion strategy in China.

Free Trade Agreements: Strategic Trade Promotion Follow-Up

Opening markets for American goods and services either through negotiating new trade agreements or through results-oriented enforcement actions is this Administration's top priority. The year 2003 was a very busy one for advancing and concluding free trade agreements (FTAs), and 2004 is shaping up to be just as important.

In 2003, the United States signed FTAs with Chile and Singapore. The U.S. Congress approved those agreements with strong bipartisan support by enacting implementing legislation. These state-of-the-art agreements set modern rules for twenty-first century commerce. In addition to lower tariffs on goods, they break new ground in such areas as services, e-commerce, intellectual property protection, transparency, and enforcement of labor and environmental laws.

Building on these agreements, the United States has already concluded another four FTAs so far this year. The Administration has reached a U.S.-Central American Free Trade Agreement (CAFTA) with five countries—El Salvador, Guatemala, Honduras, Nicaragua, and Costa Rica—and has concluded a separate but similar U.S.-Dominican Republic FTA. This group of countries would represent the second-largest U.S. export market in Latin America.

The U.S.-Australia FTA was completed in February 2004. It provides new export opportunities for the recovering manufacturing sector, as well as for agricultural and services exporters. More than 99 percent of tariffs on U.S. manufactured goods exports to Australia will be eliminated on day one—exports that account for 93 percent of total U.S. sales to Australia and support 150,000 American jobs.

> **Opening New Markets for America's Small Businesses**
>
> Ninety-seven percent of all U.S. exporters are small- and medium-sized enterprises (SMEs). Companies with fewer than 20 employees make up nearly 70 percent of all U.S. exporting firms.
>
> Small businesses may benefit the most from new trade agreements that slash foreign tariffs and remove barriers that disadvantage exporters:
>
> - More than 6,000 SMEs export to Chile
>
> - Over 4,000 SMEs export to Costa Rica
>
> - About 3,000 businesses export to Honduras

In March 2004, the United States and Morocco concluded a comprehensive free trade agreement that is another step toward a Middle East Free Trade Area, subsequent to our existing FTAs with Jordan and Israel. This agreement offers the best day-one tariff elimination in a U.S. free trade agreement with a developing country.

Strategy

Working together, the Trade Promotion Coordinating Committee (TPCC) agencies are developing a more targeted strategic approach to ensure that U.S. small businesses, manufacturers, and service sector industries benefit from these agreements. The first markets where agencies are using this approach are Chile, Singapore, the CAFTA countries, Morocco, and Australia.

For the first time, the TPCC agencies have (1) combined the analytical capability and expertise of a number of agencies and units to identify target sectors and (2) focused their programs and services to ensure U.S. companies are made aware of, and have the chance to pursue, new opportunities in FTA markets. The TPCC will apply this approach to future FTAs.

- **Priority sectors:** Agencies will combine their analytical capability, industry knowledge, and on-the-ground expertise in order to identify new opportunities and best prospect sectors for U.S. goods and services.

- **Market and sector strategies:** Agencies will work together to develop and implement strategies for assisting U.S. companies by focusing efforts in two broad areas: (1) marketing and outreach, to make sure U.S. companies understand the market and the advantages each agreement gives them; and (2) projects, trade missions, and shows, to help U.S. exporters take advantage of new opportunities from the FTAs.

FTA Outreach Through Public-Private Partnership

In fall 2003, the U.S. Chamber of Commerce was awarded a two-year Commerce Department Market Development Cooperator Program grant to implement a Free Trade Agreement Education and Trade Facilitation Project. The project seeks to raise the awareness of SMEs about the benefits of free trade agreements and exporting.

In collaboration with the Commerce Department, the U.S. Chamber of Commerce will hold seminars in communities around the country to educate SMEs, local organizations, and state officials on how to take advantage of FTAs.

The U.S. Chamber of Commerce will conduct the following activities:

- Focus on six to eight U.S. states that lack resources but have demonstrated strong support for development and implementation of a state export strategy.

- Work with the state governors, Commerce Department staff, and local chambers of commerce to enhance export assistance aimed at Western Hemisphere markets with current or planned FTAs with the United States.

- Hold two training sessions in Washington, D.C., for local-level chamber executives who are powerful export multipliers, so that they can in turn educate their local businesses and communities. An Internet-based training module is also planned.

Analytical Approach to Priority Sectors

A significant benefit of free trade agreements is the opportunity for firms to take advantage of negotiated liberalizations, including the elimination of tariff and non-tariff barriers. Combining tariff and trade data with our in-country commercial expertise, the Commerce Department has developed a new methodology to identify specific products that are "best prospects" for U.S. exports to these markets.

Using this methodology, the Commerce Department identifies products where (1) the FTA partner country (or region) has increased market access in terms of immediate or early tariff elimination and/or removal of non-tariff barriers, (2) U.S. firms are considered "competitive" based on U.S. world trade shares (that is, U.S. share of world exports of at least 10 percent), (3) there exists demand in the FTA partner's market, and (4) U.S. exports to the partner country have increased over the past few years. The product list is then vetted with industry analysts of the Manufacturing and Services unit and foreign posts of the U.S. Commercial Service in each country.

Market and Sector Strategies

Armed with a clear set of sectoral priorities and trade promotion tools, the TPCC agencies have developed a specific strategy for each FTA market that takes advantage of the unique market and benefits of each agreement while leveraging scarce resources across agencies. Rather than continue with business as usual in FTA markets, the TPCC now has a model that will focus U.S. Government promotional efforts on the most promising opportunities resulting from an FTA.

Marketing and outreach: The TPCC agencies have already started to work on an education campaign involving each FTA to raise the U.S. business community's awareness that new opportunities will exist. Because the FTAs are in various stages of completion, the outreach effort is different for each one. Since agreements with Chile and Singapore are already in force, the outreach campaign has already begun with these

TPCC Agency Tools for Marketing and Outreach

- Foreign buyer/business visitor exchanges

- FTA country domestic awareness campaigns by interagency speakers (coordinated with the Commercial Service)

- Market research

- Bilateral Web links and business-to-business venues (e.g., Export.gov, BuyUSA.gov)

- Establish government-to-government forums for identifying mutual benefits and addressing bilateral issues

- Using technology to help get the word out

TPCC Agency Tools for Projects, Trade Missions, and Shows

- Platinum Key and Gold Key Services for FTA markets

- Senior-level trade missions

- Priority sector trade events (e.g., regular trade missions, conferences)

- Major projects/infrastructure advocacy

- Trade finance solutions (e.g., credit availability, working capital, insurance, guarantees)

Platinum Key Service

The Commercial Service offers a Platinum Key Service in FTA countries. The service is designed to offer clients comprehensive, customized ways to achieve their business goals and can be as flexible as a company's objectives. Most typically the service consists of Gold Key Service-type meetings, targeted market research, seminars or workshops, and ongoing advice and assistance on the specific sector and/or project of interest to the client. The Platinum Key Service program is ideal for small or large companies that need assistance with market entry or market development, project development, and problem solving.

FTAs. Outreach efforts for the other agreements will follow. Elements of the outreach efforts include:

■ U.S. ambassadors will meet with U.S. business groups on the benefits and possibilities for increased export opportunities.

■ Officials from the Commerce Department and the Office of the United States Trade Representative (USTR) will travel domestically to talk to the U.S. business community regarding export opportunities made possible by the opening of FTA partners' markets.

■ Overseas Commercial Service officers will participate in videoconferences with companies in the United States to talk about the benefits and opportunities.

■ The Commerce Department is producing market research on each of the markets based on the sectors with the greatest opportunities.

■ Finally, the TPCC agencies are developing a calendar of trade events and activities that will raise the profile of each market and give companies an opportunity to act in a timely and effective way.

Projects, trade missions, and shows: We want to make sure U.S. exporters, particularly SMEs, have the market intelligence, matchmaking, and financing services they need to help them decide how to pursue new markets and forge business partnerships. TPCC agencies are working together to target specific events and projects where U.S. exporters will be able to advance their business. Needed services could range from recruiting for a trade mission to advocacy support.

Australia

Trade between Australia and the United States already is over $28 billion. If Australia and the United States enact the legislation necessary to implement the FTA, trade in both goods and services is expected to expand further. More than 99 percent of U.S. manufactured goods and all agricultural goods will be able to enter Australia duty free immediately. U.S. manufacturers estimate that the elimination of tariffs could result in $2 billion per year in increased exports of manufactured goods. For example, the FTA will provide duty-free access to Australia for U.S. electric motors and generators, while exports from key U.S. competitors will still be subject to 15 percent tariffs. U.S. firms currently have a 10 percent share of Australia's import market on electric motors and generators, which totaled $78 billion in 2003.

Most U.S.-manufactured goods and all agricultural goods will be able to enter Australia duty free. This is the most significant immediate reduction of industrial tariffs ever achieved in a U.S. free trade agreement. The services market has also been largely opened. The FTA will remove significant regulatory barriers, increasing market access in government procurement markets, strengthening intellectual property protection, and reducing screening barriers to U.S. investment.

Best Prospects

Best prospects for additional sales due to the FTA include: oil and gas sector equipment; professional services; broadcasting and media and film production; construction; telecommunications; biotechnology; mining equipment; information technology; broadband technologies; aerospace; electric motors and generators; and automotive parts.

Marketing and Outreach

To make U.S. companies more aware of the advantages the FTA brings and to assist smaller U.S. companies, the Commerce Department has set out a series of activities and events to help companies in these sectors.

- The Commerce Department will generate targeted market research on key sectors timed to important promotion events. For example, updated market intelligence on electric motors and generators will be available for distribution prior to the National Association of Manufacturers (NAM) 2005 show in Chicago.

- Department officials in Australia will lead an outreach effort through the Department's network of domestic offices to provide market briefs as part of seminar presentations and digital videoconferences. For example, the Department will host a series of conferences between U.S. and Australian energy companies.

Projects, Trade Shows, and Missions

- The Commerce Department will develop a series of industry-specific trade events focused on manufacturing. Examples include promoting U.S. company participation at the Australasian Oil and Gas Exhibition and Conference, to be held February 2005 in Perth. The Department will recruit U.S. companies for a U.S. auto parts trade mission to Australia to be scheduled in 2005 or 2006 and for the Australian biotech conference, Ausbiotech.

▓ The Department will propose Gold Key or Platinum Key Services for companies in FTA-advantaged sectors.

▓ The Department will bring potential Australian buyers to key U.S. trade shows, including MINExpo for mining equipment and the NAB (National Association of Broadcasters) trade show for broadcasting equipment.

Chile

U.S. products and services have traditionally sold well in Chile. However, in the late 1990s, Chile signed a series of trade agreements with Canada, Mexico, and the European Union (EU). These agreements gave products from those countries a competitive edge and were in part responsible for the U.S. share of Chile's imports dropping from 24 percent in 1997 to 17 percent in 2002. The FTA levels the playing field in Chile, giving U.S. exporters duty free access on most goods and agricultural products. The non-tariff aspects of the agreement are also important to U.S. firms. For example, U.S. firms in services sectors such as financial and electronic banking, insurance, telecommunications, database development, architecture, and engineering will benefit from increased transparency in government rules and openness to competition. Further, as government spending increases in environmental infrastructure, new opportunities will emerge for U.S. firms in environmental technology products such as solid waste and wastewater treatment products and services.

Best Prospects

Goods and services: Best prospects include 15 principal industries and service sectors in which U.S. companies have a competitive advantage and in which there are significant commercial opportunities in the Chilean market. They are: architectural and engineering services, capital markets, computer hardware and software, construction machinery and services, e-business services, environmental equipment and services (including water, air and soil treatment), food processing and packaging equipment, forestry, franchising, logistics equipment and services, medical equipment and services, mining equipment and services, power generation, safety and security equipment and services, and telecommunication equipment and services.

Agriculture: In the agricultural sector, best prospects include corn, distilled spirits in two years, and potatoes and potato products in four years. Tariff reductions in pork and pork products, beef offal, durum wheat, barley, barley malt, sorghum, soybeans and soybean meal, pasta, breakfast cereals, cereal preparations, and sunflower seeds should allow U.S. farmers increased sales. Beef is another commodity identified by USDA as having significant market potential as access on both sides will be completely liberalized over four years.

Marketing and Outreach

To make all U.S. companies more aware of the advantages the FTA brings and to help smaller U.S. companies, in particular, the TPCC agencies have a series of initiatives and activities planned in the United States.

- An ongoing series of seminars in U.S. cities will be held on sector-specific benefits of the FTA, including a series on environmental technology.

- To help exporters get accurate information on the FTA, the Commerce Department has published an on-line _Exporter's Guidebook to the U.S.-Chile Free Trade Agreement._

- Market research on all 15 of the best prospects has been completed and is available at the BuyUSA Web site (_www.BuyUSA.gov/chile/en_).

Projects, Trade Shows, and Missions

- The Departments of Agriculture and Commerce are focusing on helping U.S. companies use trade shows in Chile more effectively. USDA is conducting trade show assistance and buyer alerts, and the Commerce Department is hosting U.S. pavilions in key trade shows like Expomin (mining equipment).

- The Commerce Department is hosting trade missions in best prospect sectors such as safety and security and franchising.

- The U.S. Trade and Development Agency (USTDA) is working with USTR, the State Department, the Commerce Department office in Chile, and the Chilean Government to identify activities that will support U.S. and Chilean environmental cooperation. USTDA is also providing project planning assistance to the Chilean Ministry of Health that will help position U.S. exporters in the medical equipment market.

Success Story: Small Business Benefits from U.S.-Chile FTA

Started in 1984 in Clearwater, Florida, Project Development International (PDI) is a small company of 18 employees dedicated to innovative and effective management services for the construction industry. PDI's projects include dams, bridges, highways, rail systems, housing developments, and commercial, industrial and institutional projects, which range up to $15 billion.

In 2003, PDI started exporting know-how in construction management to Latin America, with help from the Americas Linkage Program (State of Florida) and the Commercial Service. PDI International Program Manager Roberto Sanchez traveled to Chile in May 2003 as part of an Americas Linkage trade mission. Through this program, Commercial Service staff in Santiago arranged meetings for Mr. Sanchez with several potential Chilean partners.

Three months later PDI signed a representation agreement with Integra Proyectos, a Chilean consultancy firm based in Santiago. "The Americas Linkage Program, along with the help of the U.S. Commercial Service, provides excellent assistance for small companies, like PDI, who want to export overseas," said Mr. Sanchez.

Mr. Sanchez credits much of PDI's success in the market to the U.S.-Chile FTA that went into effect in January 2004. The lowered tariffs and improved market access for U.S. suppliers have made it easier for PDI to export its services.

SBA Helps SMEs Export to Western Hemisphere

The Small Business Administration (SBA) is spearheading the creation of a Micro, Small and Medium-sized Enterprise (SME) Congress of the Americas. The SME Congress is a hemispheric network of SME service providers created to enhance the ability of small businesses to effectively participate and benefit from international trade opportunities. SBA is working closely with its counterparts in Chile, Brazil, Mexico, Costa Rica, and Canada on this initiative. The first full SME Congress meeting is scheduled to take place in Chile in late September and early October 2004. SME participation in trade will be among the issues discussed. The SME Congress is currently working with the U.S. Chamber of Commerce to identify and publicize success stories of small business trade in the Americas.

Central America

Individually, the countries of Central America are small markets. However, together they represent substantial opportunities for U.S. businesses. Under CAFTA, over 80 percent of U.S. industrial products—which have faced tariffs as high as 15 percent—will be duty free, with remaining tariffs being eliminated in 10 years. Half of the current U.S. agriculture exports to the region will be duty free, with tariffs on the remaining half being phased out over 15 years. In addition to the tariff reductions, increased competition and government transparency will provide new opportunities for U.S. services firms.

Best Prospects

Goods: Best prospects in goods are: yarn and fabric; chemicals such as insecticides, carbonates, medicaments, vitamins, and coloring matter; beauty and hair products; consumer goods including dental products, processed foods, washing machines, lamps and light fittings, furniture, and air conditioning machines; office paper products; information technology products such as optical fiber cables, and semiconductor devices; office machinery, refrigerators, freezers and heat pumps, and industrial furnaces; special purpose vehicles; environmental/pollution control technologies; construction equipment; and hotel and restaurant equipment.

Services: Best prospects in services industries include: franchising, financial services, tourism (car rental and airlines), express delivery, wireless telecommunications, advertising, and professional services (construction, architectural, and accounting).

Agriculture: Best prospects in the agriculture sector include: beef, apples, pears, grapes, raisins, cherries, peaches, cranberries and related products, frozen potato fries, frozen concentrated orange juice, sweet corn, almonds, pistachios, walnuts, wine, and whiskey. There are also duty-free tariff-rate quotas for U.S. pork, chicken leg quarters, rice, corn, and dairy products.

Marketing and Outreach

Due to the surge of interest in Central America by the U.S. exporting community, Commercial Service operations in Central America have been "regionalized," with the naming of a Regional Senior Commercial Officer and the launching of the Commercial Service's El Salvador office in November 2003. The regional team has developed a

"Destination Central America—Latin America's Newest Emerging Market" show as part of the drive to educate U.S. exporters about CAFTA. Three of the Commercial Service's Senior Commercial Officers from Central America have presented this program in over 40 cities across the United States. Upcoming events include:

- Continuation of the "Destination Central America" show across the United States, including outreach events in South Carolina, North Carolina, Mississippi, Louisiana, and California.

- Video conference on CAFTA issues and best products.

- SBA's SME Congress of the Americas initiative and work plan for bilateral cooperation.

Projects, Trade Shows, and Missions

- The Departments of Agriculture and Commerce will provide U.S. exporters with trade show support, importers' and buyers' lists, "hot export potential" alerts, and U.S. in-country assistance.

- CAFTA-related trade missions and events will take place, including a new telecommunications trade show in Costa Rica and the Material World textiles trade show in Miami.

- USTDA is providing $3.7 million in funding for nine activities throughout the region (see text box). The projects associated with these activities could lead to more than $200 million in U.S. exports.

- Ex-Im Bank will consider establishing a credit facility in support of infrastructure projects and SME development for credit-worthy borrowers.

USTDA Spotlight on CAFTA

USTDA activities in the region are dedicated to assisting in the development of regional economies as well as opening doors for U.S. companies to take advantage of this expanding market. The following sectors are priorities:

- Telecommunications regulatory reform

- Telecommunications infrastructure

- National energy policy

- Port modernization and operations efficiency

- Geothermal power generation

- Regional transportation networks

- Trade documentation efficiency

- E-government

- IT training and technology transfer

Singapore

Singapore has been one of the United States' key Asian trading partners for the last 20 years. The FTA, which went into force in January 2004, is serving to further enhance this relationship. While tariffs in Singapore are low, the FTA guarantees zero tariffs immediately on all U.S. goods, and ensures that Singapore cannot increase its duties on any U.S. product. Singapore will now treat U.S. services exactly like the services of its own suppliers. Market access in services is enhanced by the strong discipline of regulatory authority in Singapore.

Best Prospects

Best prospects as a result of the increased openness in services sectors and government procurement offers opportunities for financial services, telecommunications equipment and parts, distribution services and express delivery, healthcare services, education, construction services, and information technology including computers and parts. Enhanced protection of intellectual property will expand U.S. firms' market access in high-tech goods including satellite dishes and broadcasting equipment, microelectronics such as optical fibers and appliances, x-ray equipment, medical instruments, photo equipment, vitamins, and distilled spirits.

Marketing and Outreach

The Commerce Department is organizing seminars and speaking events to promote the benefits of using Singapore as a gateway for U.S. companies to expand into the rest of Asia. For example, the U.S. Ambassador to Singapore will travel to a number of U.S. cities to highlight the benefits of the FTA.

Projects, Trade Shows, and Missions

- The Commerce Department is beginning to recruit for trade missions in best prospect sectors. For instance, the Department is recruiting for an Information Technology and Communications (ICT) Mission to take advantage of the enhanced provisions for intellectual property rights.

- The Commerce Department is also focusing on trade shows both in the United States and Singapore where U.S. companies can meet with potential Singaporean buyers. For example, the Department is organizing a co-exhibitor program at CommunicAsia and BroadcastAsia to focus on companies in the broadcasting equipment sector.

Morocco

Morocco has been a strong trade partner for the United States. The FTA will improve U.S. exporters' goods and services competitiveness in this market. As Morocco begins implementing an Association Agreement with the EU, most EU industrial and agricultural exports to Morocco will enjoy preferential tariff treatment, putting American producers at a comparative disadvantage. Currently, U.S. goods entering Morocco face an average tariff of over 20 percent. When the U.S.-Morocco FTA is implemented, U.S. exports will receive more favorable tariff treatment. More than 95 percent of the bilateral trade in consumer and industrial goods will become duty free immediately upon the agreement's entry into force, with all remaining tariffs eliminated within nine years. Tariffs on many agricultural products will be cut significantly, and those on some products will be eliminated immediately. As with other FTAs, service providers will benefit from improved intellectual property protection, more open procurement rules, and regulatory transparency.

Best Prospects

Goods: Best prospects in information technology and consumer and industrial goods include: sound media equipment, semiconductor devices, data processing, electrical and precision instruments; hair and beauty products; chemical products such as additives, paints and varnishes, and cleaning products; industrial and electrical machinery, fork lift trucks, tractors and trailers, machine tools, construction equipment, electrical energy products; medicaments including antibiotics and hormones; aluminum; automotive accessories including electrical lighting and windshield wipers; and aircraft and spacecraft.

Services: Improved openness in services offers opportunities in: water treatment, such as wastewater and seawater desalination; tourism; engineering and consulting; and new governmental procurement opportunities in construction, financial, and professional services.

> ### U.S. Farmers' Potential Exports
>
> Areas of potential U.S. exports to Morocco's retail market are dominated by small, family-operated grocery stores and food processors. Morocco's food processing sector has a growing interest in U.S. products, such as milk powder, cheese, processed nuts, and other foodstuffs. Few processors purchase ingredients directly from exporters. To penetrate this segment of the market, USDA will assist U.S. exporters in locating local suppliers of these small enterprises in order to export through the current distribution networks.

Marketing and Outreach

- The Departments of Commerce, Agriculture, and State are developing FTA seminar programs for both the United States and Morocco. For example, the U.S. Embassy has developed road shows to Tangiers and Marrakech.

- The Commerce Department will establish a Middle East Business Information Center that will highlight market conditions and opportunities resulting from the FTA.

- The Commerce Department will develop market research on the FTA and an outreach e-mail campaign to U.S. business contacts and multipliers with potential in this market.

Projects, Trade Shows, and Missions

- TPCC agencies will coordinate trade missions to Morocco in priority services and infrastructure sectors. For instance, the Commerce Department will assist the American Chamber of Commerce in Morocco with a reverse trade mission to the United States, promoting bilateral business and economic opportunities as well as investment in Morocco.

- USTDA has targeted reverse trade missions (orientation visits) in the services and information technology sectors. The Commerce Department is organizing several other reverse trade missions in best prospects sectors.

Future Free Trade Agreement Prospects

Looking to the future, the list of negotiations soon to be launched or already underway indicates that bilateral trade agreements will continue to be a source of new, attractive opportunities and market access for U.S. exporters. The U.S. Government hopes to complete a free trade agreement with Bahrain shortly, and to begin FTA talks with Thailand in spring 2004. In Latin America, the U.S. Government will launch negotiations this spring for FTAs with Panama, Colombia, and possibly with Peru and Ecuador, while continuing preparatory work with Bolivia. Negotiations also continue with five countries of the Southern African Customs Union toward what will be the first U.S. FTA completed with countries from sub-Saharan Africa. U.S. Government agencies are working closely with their counterparts to develop a convergence of free trade principles and trade capacity building strategies that will maximize the benefit of the FTA for both developed and developing partners.

Coordination in Crisis Regions

I nteragency coordination in support of economic security policy objectives has substantially improved since the Trade Promotion Coordinating Committee's (TPCC's) 2002 report. A major concern of exporters in TPCC focus groups three years ago was the lack of coordinated U.S. Government commercial strategies in crisis regions such as Bosnia-Herzegovina. The result was lost opportunity—not only for U.S. companies that lost contracts to companies from more aggressive countries, but also for the host countries themselves—in terms of slower involvement of U.S. companies (vis-à-vis their know-how and investment) in rebuilding broken economies and infrastructure.

A Government-wide Strategy for Iraq

No national security imperative tested the ability of the agencies to respond with coordinated, targeted, and creative initiatives as did Iraq. Early on, the TPCC agencies concentrated on eliminating legislative and administrative barriers to allowing federal programs to operate in Iraq. Once the programs became operational, agencies moved quickly to help the Iraqis establish the institutions they will need for a stable and growing economy—a central goal of a unified and prosperous Iraq. The U.S. Government has also made sure U.S. companies have the very best information on business opportunities in Iraq and the assistance they need to invest in Iraq and partner with the Iraqi people.

U.S. Department of the Treasury

The Treasury Department established the Iraq Financial Task Force in early March 2003, and Treasury's Office of Technical Assistance began selecting technical advisors to deploy to Iraq as soon as conditions on the ground permitted. Treasury has worked along with other U.S. Government agencies, Coalition partners, and Iraqis in the areas of banking, monetary policy, taxation, budget, debt, shipping frozen assets, and financial crimes.

One major initiative that directly supports the TPCC's objectives was the creation of the Trade Bank of Iraq (TBI). TBI was established to facilitate efficient imports of capital goods into the country for reconstruction efforts. The Bank became officially operational on December 4, 2003. TBI operations are supported by a multinational banking consortium lead by JP Morgan Chase. The Bank has reached agreements with 16 export

Financial Reconstruction in Iraq

Reconstituting the core functions of the financial sector is critical to achieving a unified and prosperous Iraq. Thanks to the extensive advance planning and diligent work of many dedicated professionals in the United States, Coalition partners, and Iraqi officials, substantial progress has been made on financial reconstruction over the last several months. This process is helping to create the basis for a robust trade relationship between the United States and Iraq.

credit agencies to insure more than $2.4 billion dollars in Iraqi imports throughout the world.

Another key objective was developing a sound monetary framework and a stable currency in Iraq. The introduction of a new Iraqi currency was successfully completed in January 2004. The new currency, along with other monetary initiatives, will help facilitate trade between the international community and Iraq.

Treasury worked with other TPCC agencies to enact a new Foreign Investment law that allows individual foreign investors to acquire up to a 100 percent ownership in Iraqi assets. In addition, new banking laws and regulations have been created which will underpin the development of a sound, modern banking system.

Addressing Iraq's substantial foreign debt problem is crucial to the country's medium-term economic health. President Bush asked former Secretary of State James A. Baker to serve as his Special Presidential Envoy to restructure Iraq's official debt burden. With the assistance of the United States, all parties—including both members and non-members of the Paris Club—will be better able to reach a resolution on reducing Iraq's unsustainable debt burden.

Commerce Department: International Trade Administration

On-the-ground activities: The Commerce Department has had staff members in Baghdad and at the Department of Defense since late March 2003, who provide valuable support to the overall U.S. Government effort to reform the Iraqi economy. Personnel of the Commerce Department's International Trade Administration (ITA) have been serving in Baghdad as Coalition Provisional Authority (CPA) Senior Advisors to the Ministry of Trade and to the Ministry of Industry and Planning. ITA helped to create, and ITA staff has headed, the Iraqi Business Center to serve the emerging entrepreneurial spirit of the Iraqi people. ITA and National Telecommunications and Information Administration staff also provided technical experts on standards and spectrum allocation. Other in-country staff members are helping U.S. companies navigate the difficult commercial environment in Iraq and learn of potential opportunities.

- In support of Iraq reconstruction, ITA certified two trade fairs in the region. The Commerce Department sponsored the Arab Health trade event in Dubai and, with support from the Department of Health and Human Services, sponsored a 10-member Iraqi delegation to the event. Arab Health is the premier Middle East medical devices trade event. Additionally, the Commerce Department provided trade fair certification to Outreach 2004 in January 2004 in Amman, Jordan.

Outreach 2004 was a multi-sectoral trade show focused on reconstruction opportunities in Iraq.

▓ Together with Commercial Service posts in the region, including Amman, Dubai, Kuwait City, Riyadh, Istanbul, and Ankara, the Commerce Department is providing support to U.S. companies interested in doing business in Iraq through the Iraq Reconstruction Regional Initiative.

Stateside assistance for U.S. companies: In cooperation with the TPCC agencies, the Commerce Department created an Iraq Investment and Reconstruction Task Force to serve as an interagency source of information for U.S. companies interested in reconstruction and commercial opportunities. The Task Force works closely with the CPA in Iraq and in Washington, D.C., the U.S. Agency for International Development (USAID), the Overseas Private Investment Corporation (OPIC), the Export-Import Bank of the United States (Ex-Im Bank), the U.S. Trade and Development Agency (USTDA), and the U.S. Departments of Defense, State, and Treasury. The Task Force is committed to ensuring that the U.S. Government is providing the business community with the latest information on government contract opportunities and the business climate in Iraq.

Toward its primary goal of bringing opportunities closer to U.S. companies, the Task Force:

▓ Developed a comprehensive Web site resource (*www.export.gov/iraq*) where U.S. companies receive clear, accurate, and timely information about Iraq reconstruction contracts, related opportunities and resources, and the evolving commercial environment in Iraq. It provides Web site links to the CPA in Iraq, other U.S. Government agencies, reconstruction prime contractors, and known subcontractors. The Web site attracts over 40,000 visitors per month, and it received over 300,000 hits in 2003.

▓ Established an e-mail alert service for keeping companies informed about the latest opportunities and business updates available, as well as an e-mail inquiry service (*IraqInfo@mail.doc.gov*) and a toll-free hotline for businesspersons requiring additional guidance and business counseling (1-866-352-IRAQ). More than 6,200 companies from 93 countries have registered to receive *IraqAlerts*; the e-mail inquiry address receives an average of 30 or more inquiries a day.

▓ Authors the continuously updated "Business Guide for Iraq," which surveys the commercial environment in Iraq and provides analysis of leading industry sectors, and "Doing Business in Iraq—Frequently Asked Questions," which provides unique and practical information on traveling to, trading with, and investing in Iraq.

- Maintains a thorough listing of all U.S. Government reconstruction contractors and known subcontractors that suppliers and smaller companies can reference to pursue potential partnering opportunities.

- Meets with U.S. companies and other industry groups nationwide as part of an outreach campaign to involve the broad participation of small, medium, and large U.S. companies in Iraq reconstruction.

- Hosts roundtables throughout the United States for Iraqi-Americans and U.S. companies interested in the rebuilding of Iraq.

- Meets with Coalition companies and other foreign officials and industry delegations to enhance transparency and international participation by providing information on the commercial environment in Iraq and U.S. Government subcontracting opportunities.

- Sponsored a series of interagency industry briefings with senior officials from the Departments of Commerce, State, and Treasury, and from USAID, the CPA, Ex-Im Bank, OPIC, and USTDA.

Improving the commercial environment in Iraq: On the policy front, the Commerce Department has played a significant role with other agencies in assisting the CPA to make it possible for U.S. firms to establish their businesses or hire Iraqi representatives.

- The Commerce Department's ITA and Office of General Counsel have played a major role, along with other TPCC agencies, in developing the decree liberalizing investment in Iraq and have provided extensive assistance to the CPA on a wide range of initiatives seeking to improve the commercial environment in Iraq and generate new employment for the Iraqi people.[2]

- The Commerce Department is assisting the CPA and the Iraqi Ministry of Trade to make it possible for U.S. firms to establish and register their businesses.

- The Office of General Counsel has compiled extensive information on Iraqi commercial law, which has been widely disseminated by the Commerce Department through Web sites and presentations. The Office of General Counsel

---

2. Investors should keep in mind that after June 30, 2004, the people of Iraq and the government that they select will continue to re-shape Iraqi laws and policies as Iraq's economy and legal system become more sophisticated and robust. The U.S. Government expects—but cannot guarantee—that the Iraqi transitional government and the people of Iraq will continue on the path toward a free and open economy and legal system. Toward this end, the CPA, the Governing Council, the Iraqi ministries, the U.S. Government, and our coalition partners have been planning a broad range of technical assistance and capacity building programs that will give Iraq the tools it needs to build on the solid economic and legal foundations that the CPA and the Governing Council have laid.

also has provided extensive advice to American companies and attorneys seeking information about the legal aspects of doing business in Iraq.

U.S. Trade and Development Agency

There will be an important role for USTDA's commercially-oriented development assistance in Iraq. The programs of USTDA are particularly effective in bringing private sector solutions to early reconstruction efforts in post-conflict regions. This has been demonstrated successfully in Bosnia, Serbia and Montenegro, and most recently, Afghanistan.

U.S. businesses have the technology and expertise to provide much-needed assistance that will help the people of Iraq to secure an environment for social and economic stability and growth. USTDA is poised to use its experience and programs to support U.S. policy goals in Iraq through the provision of private sector solutions to the reconstruction effort.

USTDA's initial activity was an orientation visit for a delegation from the Iraq rail sector in January 2004. Severe neglect since the end of the first Gulf War, in addition to looting following the conclusion of major combat operations in the current conflict, have critically degraded the assets of the Iraqi rail sector. Reconstruction of the sector is a priority for the stabilization of the country. U.S. businesses can provide the goods and services necessary to rebuild the rail system, and the orientation visit exposed Iraqi decision-makers to U.S. private sector solutions to the challenges they face. USTDA intends for the orientation visit to be the first in a series of such activities.

USTDA has received a $5 million transfer of funds for support of activities in Iraq. Discussions are underway with the CPA and Iraqi officials on how best to utilize this funding to meet Iraqi development needs while also supporting U.S. commercial interests.

Overseas Private Investment Corporation

Congress provided OPIC with authority to open its programs in Iraq through the Iraq Supplemental Appropriations Act, which the President signed into law last autumn. OPIC's unique ability to mobilize private capital by mitigating risk makes the agency an effective tool in moving beyond simple grant assistance to genuine private sector-led economic development.

OPIC is currently seeking to augment and complement international efforts to support the reconstruction of Iraq through loan guarantee facilities that will modernize and reform the Iraqi banking sector, and by providing additional liquidity to promote private sector trade, small- and medium-sized enterprises (SMEs), and reconstruction efforts on the ground.

Additionally, OPIC's political risk insurance coverage provides critical risk mitigation that will allow American investors to establish businesses in the new Iraqi economy, promoting development and reconstruction, and the principles of free markets, rule of law, and private property that are institutional prerequisites for economic growth.

Export-Import Bank of the United States

Ex-Im Bank is committed to helping U.S. exporters participate in trade with Iraq and to assisting with Iraq reconstruction efforts. As of February 2004, Ex-Im Bank support for U.S. exports to Iraq was possible through the following means:

- In November 2003, Ex-Im Bank approved a $500 million short-term insurance facility for the TBI. Under this facility, Ex-Im Bank insures short-term letters of credit issued by, or on behalf of, TBI in support of purchases of U.S. goods and services. Ex-Im Bank, TBI, and the CPA entered into a Framework Agreement regarding the facility, which served as a model for similar arrangements with OPIC and 15 other export credit agencies. TBI is an independent Iraqi Government entity created to provide trade finance services to facilitate imports to Iraq.

- Ex-Im Bank is willing to provide working capital loan guarantees to U.S. exporters, particularly SMEs, operating under U.S. Government-funded reconstruction contracts. Ex-Im Bank's working capital guarantees permit U.S. exporters to finance their pre-export activities, which include purchasing raw materials, equipment, and supplies.

- Ex-Im Bank may also finance exports to Iraq if the repayment obligation is guaranteed or otherwise backed by a creditworthy source of repayment in a third country where Ex-Im Bank is open for business. This structure shifts the repayment risk of a transaction from Iraq to the source of repayment in the third country, enabling Ex-Im Bank to provide its support.

Ex-Im Bank also continues to work closely with the CPA and others to find ways to support larger and longer-term projects. These proposals, once implemented, could provide U.S. exporters with unprecedented opportunities to compete for sales to Iraq's expanding oil and infrastructure sectors.

Agriculture Department

The U.S. Department of Agriculture (USDA) is contributing to the Administration's objective of building a democratic Iraq with a market-based economic system. USDA has worked closely with the World Food Program (WFP) to ensure a continued supply of food to all Iraqi households and a successful transition of the Oil for Food Program. USDA has contributed to the re-establishment of the Iraqi Ministry of Agriculture and to regional authorities and has recently worked with the Ministry of Trade, which will oversee the establishment of the Iraqi import regime and food purchasing contracts.

Northern Iraq Ministry advisor: Since July 2003, a USDA employee has been in Northern Iraq assisting the CPA to transfer the management of agricultural projects worth $91 million from the Food and Agriculture Organization of the United Nations to the Regional Ministry of Agriculture. This individual will be replaced in 2004, and will be joined by three specialists in irrigation, animal disease control, and plant protection.

Agricultural advisor in Baghdad: Early in the reconstruction phase of the war, USDA placed an agricultural advisor in Baghdad to assist in reconstituting the Ministry of Agriculture under the guidance of the CPA. In July 2003, the first USDA representative returned to the United States and was replaced by a second USDA employee. The goal of the representative is to assist with recreating a functioning Ministry of Agriculture and with the transition of the United Nations contracts to the Ministry.

Small Business Administration

The Small Business Administration (SBA) has detailed an employee to Iraq as part of the Iraqi rebuilding effort. The employee will be interacting with the Iraqi provisional government's Ministry of Finance in the planning and development of a small business agency to support Iraqi entrepreneurs and the SME sector.

U.S. Department of Labor

The Department of Labor is supporting reconstruction efforts in Iraq by providing both human and monetary resources. During her visit to Iraq in January 2004, Secretary of Labor Chao participated in the grand opening of the Baghdad Employment Center, one of 28 scheduled to open by June 2004. Over the past year, the Department has posted three officials as advisors to the CPA and Iraqi government on labor issues. The Department is funding a $5 million project to reintegrate ex-combatants into civil society and create and build the capacity of employment services throughout Iraq. The employment centers will help link jobseekers with employers who need workers, and provide other services such as job counseling and skills training. The Department is also funding a scholarship program designed to increase labor market information capacity, teach participants how to gather information on worker rights' indicators, and increase the Department's access to accurate and complete workforce and economic data. Iraqi participants in the next training session are expected to be women.

USTDA Focus on Transportation Security

In today's post-September 11 environment, the international transportation system is as important to economic efficiency as it is to national security. The key to addressing both concerns is the effective tracking of goods through the global transportation system. Through its work in the Asia-Pacific region, and now throughout the world, USTDA is taking a leadership role in introducing strategies for supply chain security and transportation logistical systems.

The 2003 National Export Strategy noted USTDA's work in the Pacific Rim countries, highlighted by the official launch of the Secure Trade in the APEC Region (STAR) initiative in February 2003 in Bangkok, Thailand. Over the past year, USTDA has expanded this work to Africa, the Middle East, and South Asia. For example, in February 2004, USTDA, in cooperation with the U.S. Departments of Homeland Security, Transportation, and Commerce, held a regional forum on trade and transportation security in Cairo, Egypt. At the African Growth and Opportunity Act (AGOA) Forum in December 2003, USTDA sponsored the workshop "Bringing Transportation Security into the AGOA Framework."

A Government-wide Strategy for Afghanistan

The U.S. Government announced a new initiative in October of 2003 to accelerate reconstruction in Afghanistan. A major component of that strategy is to help create economic opportunities for Afghans through the establishment of a thriving private sector that is linked to the rest of the world through trade.

State Department

Acting as the coordinating agency in Afghanistan for the U.S. Government, State works to set the broad policy parameters. State is also working to restore Afghanistan's role as a key transit country linking Central Asia with South Asia. Reopening these historic trade routes through Afghanistan has the potential of increasing prosperity for both Afghanistan and the wider region.

The State Department assisted the Afghan Government in organizing a March 2004 international conference at which the donor community was asked to continue its support to Afghanistan's reconstruction, with a particular focus on private sector initiatives.

Department of the Treasury

The Iraq and Afghanistan Financial Task Force coordinates the Treasury Department's efforts on Afghanistan. Through the Task Force, Treasury has been an outspoken advocate for sound economic policies. For example, Treasury initiated the Administration's proposal to establish industrial parks that will provide infrastructure essential to private sector development. Treasury's Office of Technical Assistance has provided technical advisors on debt and budget issues, and Treasury was instrumental in designing some of the necessary regulations for an effective financial sector. This is helping to lay the foundation for the government to attract investment and provide services to the private sector.

Overseas Private Investment Corporation

As part of the U.S. Government's commitment to the post-Taliban government under the leadership of President Karzai, OPIC has extended a $100 million line of credit to promote private sector investment in Afghanistan. In 2003, OPIC concluded agreements that provided $40 million in financing and insurance to a U.S consortium that will construct an international hotel in Kabul. The project represents the largest single U.S. private investment in Afghanistan since the fall of the Taliban regime. Indeed, it is the largest U.S. investment in a generation or more.

Moreover, OPIC will provide $5 million in political risk insurance for Shelter FOR Life International, Inc. to help rebuild Afghanistan's infrastructure, through repair of existing roads, construction of housing and schools, and development of water supply systems. A $3 million OPIC loan will enable a U.S. small business owned by an Afghan-American to provide significant seasonal employment for Afghan women.

Additional pipeline projects in banking and housing are under way.

U.S. Trade and Development Agency

Afghanistan is an example of how USTDA can move quickly to respond to U.S. foreign policy and strategic objectives, while supporting both economic development and U.S. commercial interests. In the past two years, USTDA has provided $3.5 million in assistance in the Afghan telecommunications, oil and gas, power, civil aviation, tourism, and education sectors. In 2003, USTDA utilized the full range of its activities in Afghanistan. The highlight of USTDA's 2003 Afghan program was the "Afghanistan: Rebuilding a Nation" conference the agency co-sponsored with the Commerce Department (see text box). Already, USTDA policy-oriented work in Afghanistan, particularly in the telecommunications sector, is bearing fruit with the launch of a new cellular network in the summer of 2003.

In September 2003, USTDA Director Askey traveled to Afghanistan with Treasury Secretary Snow, where she announced an Industrial Capacity and Market Development Initiative. This initiative will help to develop local capacity in manufacturing, assembly, and services, and will support Afghanistan's efforts to improve its physical infrastructure and human resource base. In the coming year, this will be complemented by USTDA's program in the oil and gas sector, which consists of a feasibility study on a domestic natural

> ### USTDA and the Commerce Department Organize Major Business Conference
>
> In June 2003, USTDA and the Commerce Department co-sponsored the "Afghanistan: Rebuilding a Nation" conference, which drew over 430 participants, including over 300 U.S. company representatives. The conference opened with the reading of a letter from President Bush and a videotaped greeting from Afghan President Karzai. Key Afghan ministers and officials addressed the conference and presented specific information on approximately 35 projects. Project opportunities included the following sectors: construction, transportation, water and sanitation, telecommunications, oil and gas, and power.

49

gas pipeline and a hydrocarbon resource survey, both of which are currently underway. This sector represents one of Afghanistan's best chances of attracting foreign investment and alleviating its energy crisis, and it is also a significant commercial opportunity for U.S. companies. Additional activities are likely to focus on the aviation and construction materials sectors.

Commerce Department: International Trade Administration

The Commerce Department created the Afghanistan Investment and Reconstruction Task Force in February 2002 to respond to strong private sector interest in participating in reconstruction activities. The Task Force also represents the Commerce Department and ITA at U.S. Government interagency policy meetings as a representative of private sector interests.

On-the-ground activities: The Task Force works closely with a foreign service national (funded by USTDA) in Kabul to coordinate commercial activities and assist U.S. companies. The Task Force also works closely with the Ministry of Commerce and other parts of the Afghan Government.

The Commerce Department has conducted two policy missions to Afghanistan and plans a third. In August 2002, the Department led an interagency mission that included representatives from OPIC and USTDA. Secretary Evans visited in October 2003 to underscore the Administration's commitment to Afghanistan's rebuilding efforts. In April 2004, Assistant Secretary of Commerce Lash will visit Afghanistan to emphasize investment opportunities.

Stateside assistance for U.S. companies: The Task Force serves as a central information resource for U.S. companies interested in commercial opportunities in Afghanistan, coordinating closely with TPCC agencies. Among other activities, the Task Force:

- Gathers and disseminates current information on investment and reconstruction activities by phone, e-mail, or through the Web site (*www.export.gov/afghanistan*).

- Provides business counseling to U.S. companies.

- Coordinates major events. In 2003, events included the "Afghanistan: Rebuilding a Nation" conference and roundtables in New York, California, Texas, and Washington, D.C. These roundtables reached hundreds of Afghan-American citizens who have a keen interest in rebuilding Afghanistan.

Improving the trade and investment policy environment: ITA has been instrumental in expanding bilateral commercial and trade relations between the United States and Afghanistan through:

- Working closely with the Office of the U.S. Trade Representative to expedite the review process for extending preferential duty treatment to Afghan goods under the U.S. Generalized System of Preferences (GSP) program, which went into effect in January 2003.

- Coordinating with the Commerce Department's Commercial Law Development Program in April 2003 to train the Afghan Government and private traders on the GSP program and other U.S. import regulations.

- Working through the U.S. Embassy in Kabul with the Ministry of Commerce and the newly created Afghanistan Investment Support Agency to improve the commercial environment in Afghanistan.

- Cooperating with the National Institute of Standards and Technology and the Food and Drug Administration to assess the standards infrastructure needs of the Afghan Government and to bring training and capacity to Afghanistan's nascent standards infrastructure.

U.S. Agency for International Development

USAID is working to improve economic governance in Afghanistan in order to increase private sector investment and economic growth. A foundation for this work was the conversion of the national currency, which USAID assisted the Central Bank in implementing in late 2002 and early 2003.

Recent progress with the Central Bank includes:

- Establishing national and international money transfer services.

- Creating and implementing commercial banking regulations and licensing (three commercial banks have been established in Afghanistan to date).

- Implementing monetary policy (the new currency has maintained its value since its introduction).

Recent progress with the Ministry of Finance includes:

- Customs: Implementing streamlined customs in Kabul posts; designing a customs reform program; and beginning customs reform at four posts outside Kabul.

- Budget: Assisting in developing the first national budget and in developing capabilities for next year's budget.

▓ Assisting in placing the central government in control of provincial budget execution through Ministry of Finance representatives (Mustofiats).

▓ Tax administration: Designing and implementing the issuance of tax identification numbers; working to implement the Large Taxpayer Officer.

USAID continues to work with relevant ministries in trade reform and public utilities.

Agriculture Department

Secretarial visit: Agricultural Secretary Veneman traveled to Kabul in November 2003 to directly observe the problems and progress of agricultural reconstruction in Afghanistan. In meeting with President Karzai, Secretary Veneman reinforced the U.S. commitment to the Karzai government and the rehabilitation of Afghanistan.

Cochran Fellowships: Also in November 2003, Secretary Veneman announced a program to provide Cochran Fellowships for Afghan women and allow eight women annually to receive training in the United States on how to finance agricultural production. The women are scheduled to come to the United States in April 2004.

Provincial Reconstruction Teams: At the request of the Department of Defense, three USDA employees were sent to Afghanistan in September and October 2003 to serve for six months as civilian agricultural advisors on Provincial Reconstruction Teams.

Afghan Conservation Corps: At the request of the State Department, USDA employees are periodically sent to Kabul to assist the Afghan Conservation Corps in achieving its goal of implementing conservation projects using labor-intensive methods that put cash into the hands of the rural population.

Public Law (P.L.) 480: USDA provided food for distribution immediately following the fall of the Taliban regime and continues to monitor Afghan food needs. More recently, governmental or non-governmental organizations are selling surplus USDA commodities to generate funds for development projects. A P.L. 480 program has been established with the Afghan Government under which donated soybean oil is being sold, with the proceeds earmarked for rural development projects. Some 4,200 tons ($5 million worth) of vegetable oil were delivered in December 2003. The Secretary has announced that another 4,200 tons of vegetable oil will be delivered in 2004.

U.S. Department of Labor

The Department of Labor is funding two programs in Afghanistan:

- A $3 million vocational training project focuses on improving the social and economic status of vulnerable groups in Afghan society. Activities include market-based vocational apprenticeships and skills training, as well as development of an employer network with medium to large businesses.

- A $300,000 income generation and skills training project teaches Afghan women to sew school uniforms for girls who cannot afford to purchase or make their own uniforms, simultaneously providing an opportunity for girls to attend school and for women to develop valuable job skills.

Ex-Im Bank in Pakistan

Pakistan has been a valuable partner of the United States in bringing peace and prosperity to Afghanistan. As such, it has been an Administration priority for the trade promotion and finance agencies to expand their efforts in Pakistan to address critical developmental needs and to encourage greater involvement of U.S. industry. Ex-Im Bank has been particularly active in this important market.

As of March 11, 2004, Ex-Im Bank has been open for short-, medium-, and long-term financing in the sovereign sector in Pakistan. Ex-Im Bank financing now will be available to support Pakistan's purchases of U.S. equipment and services in cases where repayment of the financing is assured by the sovereign guarantee of the Government of Pakistan.

The expanded coverage is a result of an upgrade in Pakistan's risk rating by the U.S. Interagency Country Risk Assessment System (ICRAS). This interagency group determines country risk ratings used for all U.S. Government international loans, guarantees, and insurance.

Aircraft: In February 2003, Ex-Im Bank authorized a Final Commitment and a Preliminary Commitment totaling more than $1.1 billion in loan guarantees in support of the export of eight U.S.-manufactured Boeing 777 aircraft, General Electric spare engines, and related spare parts to Pakistan International Airlines (Pakistan's government-owned national airline). At the time Ex-Im Bank authorized these transactions, it was closed for routine trade finance transactions in Pakistan. Nonetheless, by structuring this aircraft financing transaction as an asset-based finance lease— and because of the reduction in risk in the transaction as a result of Pakistan's ratification and implementation of the Cape Town Convention on International Interests in Aircraft Equipment—Ex-Im Bank was able to conclude that the transaction provided a reasonable assurance of repayment.

The Final Commitment will support the export of the first three Boeing 777 aircraft and related spare engines, which will be delivered during 2004. When converted into a Final Commitment, the Preliminary Commitment will support the export of five additional Boeing 777 aircraft scheduled to be delivered from 2006 through 2008.

A Government-wide Strategy for Central and Eastern Europe and Eurasia

Supporting the economic development of Central and Eastern Europe and Eurasia is of critical importance to the United States. Prosperity cements democratic reforms and promotes political and economic stability throughout these dynamic regions. In addition, it creates greater opportunities for U.S. exporters and investors. To reach this goal, U.S. Government agencies must continue to coordinate their efforts to promote free market reforms and efficient, growing economies.

Central and Eastern Europe: The United States has undertaken a special effort to strengthen the economies of the countries of Central and Eastern Europe. These efforts will be continued. Each of these countries has indicated that attracting additional U.S. investment and expanding trade with the United States are key foreign policy goals. At the same time, an important goal remains ensuring that the U.S. Government provides support for U.S. businesses as a number of the countries accede to the European Union (EU) this year and others continue accession negotiations. Over the last year, the United States has contributed to expanded commercial relations with these countries by intensifying the activities of various TPCC agencies and by launching new TPCC initiatives for Central and Eastern Europe.

Eurasia: Developing commercial opportunities in the former Soviet republics of Eurasia will also require continuing effort. In countries transitioning to more transparent market environments, the sustained involvement of the U.S. mission is often crucial in closing on export sales, ensuring access for U.S. exporters, and supporting fair resolution of commercial disputes. Most of the Eurasian countries have reversed their post-independence economic contraction and have started to achieve economic growth, most notably in the private sector. State Department FREEDOM Support Act funding provides assistance to foster this change and offers opportunities for U.S. firms to contribute and benefit from the evolution. Throughout the region, the United States has also partnered with the European Bank for Reconstruction and Development (EBRD) to support micro- and small-business lending, leading to additional export opportunities. A U.S. Government investment of $71.3 million has leveraged nearly $600 million in capital from other donors for micro- and small-business lending in 13 countries.

U.S. Trade and Development Agency

Central and Eastern Europe: USTDA remains deeply engaged in the countries of Central and Eastern Europe. Romania was named USTDA's 2003 Country of the Year thanks to the marked success of that country's USTDA program last year. USTDA Director Askey traveled to Romania in December 2003 to present the award to Romanian President Ion Iliescu. Growth and investment have increased across the region, and the EU accession of 10 new members is all but complete. This award is yet another indication that Romania and other countries in the region are "coming of age."

USTDA invested roughly $8 million in Central and Eastern Europe during FY 2003. Aviation safety and security support for Poland, Bulgaria, and Romania were among the Agency's priority investments in the region this year. In another priority area, USTDA is helping its partners improve their environmental performance, in particular by funding studies of renewable energy projects. A highlight of this effort was a Prague conference in early FY 2003 that focused on waste-to-energy and renewable energy opportunities.

Central and Eastern Europe will remain a major part of the USTDA program during 2004. The agency will be active in the Balkans and intends to continue to welcome project proposals in the new EU member states after their accession in May 2004.

Eurasia: In the Eurasia region, USTDA's 2003 program continued to advance a number of important U.S. foreign policy goals, including reconstruction efforts in Afghanistan and the establishment of market economies in the countries of the former Soviet Union. USTDA invested roughly $9 million in the region during FY 2003. Regional projects continued to be important in Eurasia in 2003, including the continuation of support for the Baku-Tbilisi-Ceyhan Oil Pipeline and the Shah Deniz Gas Pipeline projects. These projects will stimulate the economies of the countries involved, which include Azerbaijan, Georgia, and Turkey, and will help guarantee their independence and territorial integrity.

In Russia, USTDA reached out to diverse sectors of the economy. Support included technical assistance in drafting new ports legislation, a seminar on medical/pharmaceutical standards, and assistance related to establishing a legal regime for aircraft leasing. Following a banner year in 2002, USTDA remained active in Central Asia in 2003, with projects in Uzbekistan on aircraft co-production, airport security, and water resources, and in Kyrgyzstan on gold mining. In the Caucasus, USTDA funded technical assistance for the restructuring of SOCAR—Azerbaijan's state-owned oil company, a feasibility study on establishing an MBA program in Baku, and a feasibility study on a satellite earth station project in Armenia.

Success Story: USTDA Helps Small U.S. Printing and Publishing Manufacturers Sell in New Markets

At the initiative of the NPES (the Association for Suppliers of Printing, Publishing, and Converting Technologies), USTDA sponsored an orientation visit for Russian, Ukrainian, and Uzbek officials to attend Print 2001 in Chicago for an introduction to U.S. companies and technologies in the printing and publishing sector. Because of the large number of potential end users, most offering relatively small marketing opportunities, USTDA and NPES developed the innovative strategy of focusing primarily on host country sales agents or distributors. This approach was intended to build upon the distributors' existing knowledge and networks, and to show distributors that it would be in their interest to use their knowledge of host country end users to bring Russian, Ukrainian, and Uzbek buyers together with U.S. equipment makers.

The strategy is already showing success. Initial information indicates that, so far, more than 20 U.S. suppliers have sold over $5 million worth of this kind of equipment through these channels. Moreover, most U.S. producers in this sector are relatively small and would normally be unable to aggressively market their products in such distant and risky markets. The project's initial success has already led to a second USTDA technical assistance grant to NPES that supports a training center to promote sales of U.S. printing and publishing equipment in these markets.

Overseas Private Investment Corporation

To strengthen the economic relationship between the United States and the countries of Central and Eastern Europe, OPIC sponsored an investment conference in March 2004 in Bucharest, Romania. The conference, "Forging New Partnerships in Emerging Europe," attracted more than 350 participants including representatives from 15 countries and regions, U.S. Government trade and investment agencies, local and American businesses, international financial institutions, and both the President and Prime Minister of Romania.

With over 80 U.S. businesses in attendance, the conference provided a unique opportunity for officials from Albania, Bosnia and Herzegovina, Bulgaria, Croatia, the Czech Republic, Estonia, Hungary, Kosovo, Latvia, Lithuania, Macedonia, Poland, Romania, Serbia and Montenegro, Slovakia, and Slovenia to highlight investment opportunities in their countries. Conference speakers also included representatives of U.S. businesses active in the region who shared their first hand experience in sectors such as housing, telecommunications, tourism, and infrastructure. There was also a special focus on small business as well as a roundtable composed of representatives from the American Chambers of Commerce in the region. To encourage joint partnerships between American and local businesses from the region, special matchmaking meetings were organized for participants.

Export-Import Bank of the United States

Over the past four years, Ex-Im Bank has authorized financing of approximately $1.3 billion in exports to the countries of Southeast Europe and $250 million in exports to the countries of Central Europe. During this time, the SEED[3] Program has supported Ex-Im Bank's marketing and outreach activities, including a regional office in Zagreb, Croatia, established in August 2002. Although this office will be closed in 2004, Ex-Im Bank is ready to continue its commitment to the region, building on the experience and accomplishments of the Zagreb office.

Major outreach events sponsored by Ex-Im Bank include a Regional Environmental Conference held in Budapest, Hungary, in September 2002, and a Regional Finance Conference held in Bled, Slovenia, in October 2003. Although the primary focus of both conferences was Southeast Europe, delegates from Central Europe were also invited to attend.

During 2003, Ex-Im Bank held or participated in several country-specific seminars in Bulgaria, Romania, Bosnia-Herzegovina, and Serbia and Montenegro that successfully increased knowledge of Ex-Im Bank's programs, particularly among private sector companies. The seminars were organized with the assistance and backing of the U.S.

3. Support for East European Democracy (SEED) Act of 1989

embassies in the various countries through the U.S. Commercial Service offices. USTDA and OPIC were also invited to participate in these events.

This activity has resulted in a significant prospective pipeline of business for Ex-Im Bank in excess of $1 billion involving transactions in both the public and private sector. Although Ex-Im Bank does not expect that all of this potential business will result in authorized transactions, it is a clear indication of the awareness and interest in Ex-Im Bank financing. For example, Ex-Im Bank has been approached to support two major infrastructure projects in Albania, both of which are very important to the future development of the country. These represent the two most important projects involving U.S. companies in Albania. Likewise, Ex-Im Bank's activities in Romania have shown tremendous growth over the past year, and that growth is expected to continue into coming years. Ex-Im Bank stands out among export credit agencies as a significant source of long-term infrastructure financing.

Ex-Im Bank intends to continue to host both regional finance conferences and country-specific seminars. Ex-Im Bank is also seeking to establish relationships with local commercial banks that would make its programs more accessible to SMEs.

Over the next year, Ex-Im Bank will increase its marketing efforts in Central Europe. Since many of these countries are on the path to EU integration and have access to long-term financing at attractive interest rates, there is not the same level of need for Ex-Im financing in this region. However, there should be opportunities to support private sector transactions or large projects in the pubic sector for which financing is needed to meet foreign competition.

Appendix A: Final Progress Report on the 2002 Recommendations

Recommendations	Status
Early Project Development	
Formalize cooperation to develop projects in pilot countries.	New Ex-Im Bank early letter of interest (LI) developed; marketing plan for LI coordinated between Ex-Im Bank and CS. Ex-Im Bank and USTDA early project development carried out in Mexico, Brazil, and Russia. Ex-Im Bank/DOC Advocacy Center MOU: automatic referral process and expedited review for securing LIs. Next steps: Begin using early LI; promote its use in key CS posts.
Agencies will build cross-training and personnel infrastructure.	Detailees sent from CS to USTDA, OPIC. New level of coordination has been established between Ex-Im Bank and pilot CS posts.
Tied and Untied Aid	
Pilot USTDA front-end engineering and design (FEED) studies program.	In September 2002, Japan committed to untie FEED studies, so the USTDA pilot study was unnecessary. U.S. engineering and design firms have been advised to notify the U.S. Government of any potential implementation issues of this agreement.
Pilot project to use mixed credits in certain middle-income countries.	Identified scope; established procedures; identified project (wind-generated power plant in Guatemala). Next step: Implement the project.
Use War Chest to leverage OECD agreement on untied aid disciplines.	The Japanese have shown willingness to negotiate on transparency, but not yet finalized.
Use the War Chest against the unfair use of tied aid.	Ex-Im Bank and Treasury continue to monitor foreign tied aid practices and matched one foreign tied aid offer last year and deterred a second.
Market Windows	
Commission a study of the impact on U.S. exporters of competitor-country market windows.	Ex-Im Bank and DOC jointly commissioned a study of market windows that was conducted by MIT. The study results were inconclusive due to lack of hard/documented data provided by the relevant ECAs and affected U.S. exporters. Absent documented information about unfair competitive practices, there is very little appetite within the OECD for separate market window disciplines at this time. The United States continues to closely monitor market window activity, with Ex-Im Bank undertaking efforts to develop hard data on the use of market windows by ECAs going forward.
Advocacy for the Life of a Project	
Coordinate support throughout the life of viable projects.	Advocacy Center will be integrated into the CS. Trade Compliance Center outreach and casework has been coordinated with the CS.

Recommendations	Status
Crisis Regions TPCC will serve as a coordinating entity available to national security policymakers for post-crisis situations.	In Iraq: High-level coordination of on-the-ground activities, stateside assistance and outreach, and policy environment assistance are ongoing. USTDA orientation visits and IT sector activities. OPIC loan guarantee facilities. Treasury and Ex-Im Bank support of Trade Bank of Iraq. In Afghanistan: USTDA has conducted orientation visits, feasibility studies, and definitional missions. USTDA/DOC co-sponsored "Afghanistan: Rebuilding a Nation" conference. DOC Reconstruction Task Force outreach including information services, roundtables, and conferences. USTR trade policy for Afghanistan. In Central and Eastern Europe and Eurasia: TPCC initiatives and agencies' activities in transition economies and countries affected by regional conflicts are continuing.
Cross-Promotion OPIC/SBA cooperative agreement to streamline approval processes.	Cooperative agreement signed. SBA staff detailed to OPIC. OPIC has streamlined SME approvals.
OPIC/DOC cooperative agreement to jointly promote OPIC to SMEs.	Cooperative agreement signed.
Coordinate technology procurement.	Established e-government working group. Merged FAS online marketplace with BuyUSA.gov. Interagency IT procurements.
Create online registration form for use by all TPCC agencies.	Form posted and in use.
Create a shared client database.	Agencies have developed shared interagency marketing database.
CS will provide complete solutions focused on enhancing a firm's global competitiveness.	With ITA reorganization, there will be a broadened focus of CS programs.

Recommendations	Status
Available/Effective Finance	
SBA's Export Express will be expanded to $250,000 as a pilot.	Program limit has been expanded to $250,000.
Integrate Ex-Im Bank's and SBA's working capital programs.	Ex-Im Bank and SBA will sign co-guarantee agreement; co-guarantee application is being modified.
Ex-Im Bank and SBA joint marketing.	Joint mailings, symposia, and training have been undertaken and continue.
Streamline Finance/Investment	
Ex-Im Bank and OPIC will streamline processing times, where appropriate.	Ex-Im Bank implemented organizational changes to make itself more market-focused and customer-driven; engaged a process engineering team to reduce transaction processing time. OPIC created the Small Business Center to provide streamlined, "one-stop shopping" for SMEs and to reduce processing cycle time.
Ex-Im Bank electronic access to export credit insurance services.	Revamping of financial processing systems to allow online application and facilitate case processing.
Ex-Im Bank will expand its information database for repeat customers.	Ex-Im Bank organizational changes implemented to streamline processing efficiency for repeat customers.
OPIC/Ex-Im Bank cooperative agreement.	Ex-Im Bank/OPIC agreement completed to share resources on transactions processes (e.g., legal) as appropriate.
Information	
DOC will improve market research using technology solutions for collaboration between agencies.	ITA reorganization will establish a coordinated process for conducting market research.
Improve search capacity and interagency portal access.	Search engine installed; content management tool established.
Gather user feedback on access to Export.gov.	Usability test completed; changes implemented.
Ex-Im Bank use of Internet to improve access to working capital program.	Pilot finished. Delegated Authority lenders on system.
TIC will use advanced customer relationship technology.	Trade Information Center (TIC) merging with CS to bring call centers closer to field operations.

Recommendations	Status
Interagency Training	
Cross-train TPCC agency personnel and implement joint training agreement.	Developed TPCC Interagency Trade Officer Training Program—three pilot sessions completed in FY 2003; cost-sharing MOU signed; three sessions planned in FY 2004. State Department's Foreign Service Institute developed new course open to all government agencies.
CS trade finance training.	SBA training of CS senior commercial officers and foreign service nationals is ongoing.
Certify TPCC trade specialists to act as account managers.	NASBITE is incorporating CS input into its development of a trade specialist certification program.
Enhance training for state and local partners.	State/local officials have been included in TPCC Interagency Trade Officer Training Program. California State trade partners (both public and private sector) training developed.
Services	
Ex-Im Bank will adapt its programs for exporters of services.	Ex-Im Bank will evaluate the extent to which it may need to make changes to its programs and policies to meet the unique needs of the service sector. Ex-Im Bank Technology Industry Initiative: Ex-Im Bank met with major information technology companies to identify obstacles that inhibit the ability to secure Ex-Im Bank financing and explore ways in which Ex-Im Bank could address these impediments.
DOC's Advocacy Center will redesign its questionnaire for service exporters.	Redesigned questionnaire to include question on service exports.
Encourage public-private partnerships for travel and tourism sector.	DOC MOU with Japan established a public-private partnership council led by industry. Interagency training and cooperation to improve the products and services available to the services sector. State (with DOT and DOC, and supported by U.S. and foreign private sectors) is to continue encouraging foreign governments (including target markets such as China, India, Russia) to liberalize aviation markets—preferably with Open Skies agreements.
USTDA will work with service sector companies and associations.	USTDA held conferences on Eurasian tourism (with DOC, Ex-Im Bank, OPIC) and on e-government in emerging markets (with State). USTDA sponsored multiple activities to promote transportation safety and security-related services. USTDA is funding technical assistance (working with USAID) to advance export of U.S. financial services.

Recommendations	Status
Outreach/Education	
Create unified marketing materials for core TPCC agencies.	Institutionalized coordination through the interagency marketing task force. The focus has been on joint seminars, direct mail, interagency pavilions, and unified literature.
Establish tighter linkages with state export promotion agencies, including packages of federal services and joint strategic planning.	Joint state-federal programs are being developed in several states. California model launched, which includes public-private partnerships, overseas support (i.e., Platinum Key Service), joint training, and trade financing solutions.
Expand trade education efforts for new-to-export firms.	DOC conducted survey and analyzed results of SBA's E-TAP program. Survey pointed to demand for an on-line offering. SBA is exploring options for developing an on-line component to E-TAP.
Develop outreach strategy for intermediaries and logistics firms.	TPCC Secretariat staff conducted focus groups with intermediaries. DOC/ITA reorganization (putting export trading company affairs marketing under the new Assistant Secretary for Trade Promotion) should address outreach.
Integrate export control training by BIS and other agencies.	Regular interagency federal regulations seminars are ongoing.
Agriculture Initiatives (USDA led)	
New Agriculture Global Market Strategy.	Market strategy developed at conference/workshop with industry and program participants and based on input from FAS posts worldwide. Initial draft plan for the Global Market Strategy was reviewed and approved by participants of FAS market development programs and final draft progress was presented to Congressional staffers by late 2003. Current draft of the plan is under senior executive review.
Pursue long-term capacity building efforts.	During FY 2002 and 2003, USDA implemented 1,051 activities annually in support of long-term trade capacity building for developing countries and emerging markets. Direct resources expended on all activities totaled $58.3 million. Program partners included USAID, USDA's Emerging Markets Program, and State Department, among others. The activities supported sustainable infrastructure in the following strategy areas: Trade and Investment; Research and Education; Sustainable Food Systems; and the Environment.
Implement a biotech strategy aimed at coalition building and resolving market access issues.	A new Biotech Staff is fully hired and equipped. Annual reporting instructions to overseas FAS posts include mandatory monitoring and reporting on foreign country biotech issues and situation analysis. Multi-agency cooperation on foreign-country policy and education activities is underway on sound science and biotech acceptance. Importer barriers are already beginning to relax and further successes are anticipated in 2004 and 2005.

Recommendations	Status
New Exporter Assistance (USDA led)	
Implement a new processed foods division that will interface closely with the Commercial Service.	A review of processed food types and categories has resulted in re-categorizing a number of U.S. exporter trade organizations for the purpose of realigning FAS staff and service responsibilities to better serve these organizations under a single, more focused division. This realignment is underway. An official name for the processed foods division will be approved after the reorganization and consolidation of USDA services for processed food industry organizations are completed in 2005.
Improve coordination of outreach activities in the United States with other TPCC agencies.	Between January 2002 and March 2004, USDA increased its outreach activities that incorporate other federal agencies; our most notable partners are DOC and SBA. Cooperation between USDA and DOC has resulted in an MOU on the coordination of trade assistance responsibilities and a set of Standard Operating Procedures that now apply both domestically and internationally. Joint activities include participation in seminars and conferences during 2003 in over 10 states representing all the major regions of the United States. Information on multi-agency trade assistance programs is available at all USDA sponsored domestic trade shows, over a dozen a year in 2002 and 2003. USDA staff participated in all three sessions of the TPCC Interagency Trade Officer Training Program begun in 2003, and will do so again in 2004. Starting in 2001, USDA and DOC established a close working relationship on joint activities under the AgTeam concept in California. California was selected as the initial model to fully develop this effort. The effort is a huge success and is now in various stages of development throughout the United States.
Revise criteria for the branded promotion program to allow participation of medium-sized firms.	Completed. Both small and medium-sized firms are eligible to participate in the branded program.
Establish new, customized, fee-based services for exporters.	After a thorough examination, FAS has determined that the statutory requirements present an administrative challenge too complex to overcome in a practical or effective manner. Therefore, FAS cannot administer a variable reimbursement rate.
Export Finance Assistance (USDA led)	
Assess changes to improve customer service and management of the Commodity Credit Corporation (CCC), and investigate and assess the benefits of changing foreign content requirement for USDA export financing.	The assessment and investigation were compiled into a single 40 page report, completed in October 2003, which evaluated the following questions: • Investigate a public-private partnership between the CCC program and a private U.S. insurance company to allow USDA to offer a larger array of export assistance products; • Assess the potential of doing revolving credits and risk analysis on a portfolio basis instead of on a transaction-by-transaction basis to allow for increased flexibility in the program while maintaining sound management control;

Recommendations	Status
	• Determine the impact of a risk-based fee structure instead of the current flat fee structure. While this could potentially increase overall fees to exporters, it better reflects the approach of other export credit agencies and private sector lenders; • Review CCC's third country bank approval policy to potentially apply "standard practice arrangements" with banks outside the country or region of sales. This could bring about more interest in third country banking, particularly by larger multinational banks; • Investigate the benefits of raising the foreign content requirement above 10 percent for exports receiving financing (guarantees). In other countries, foreign content as high as 50 percent is allowed (Japan), placing U.S. exports at a significant disadvantage.
Provide guarantees on electronic payment mechanisms and support non-traditional letter-of-credit forms.	FAS has developed an electronic database system over the past two years; development is in its final stages. This system is intended to permit exporters and their assignees to perform most functions electronically: qualify as a program participant; apply for guarantee coverage; amend payment guarantees; submit assignment notifications; submit and/or amend evidence of export reports; submit notices of nonpayment; and submit withdrawals of notices of nonpayment. Furthermore, electronic messaging will soon be available for an array of program communications, from notification of eligibility under the commercial export credit guarantee programs to issuance of payment guarantees. Additional e-government initiatives are being explored to further enhance customer service and cost-efficient program operations.

Appendix B: TPCC Program Budget Authority

TPCC Program Budget Authority, Fiscal Years 2003–2005 (millions of dollars)

	FY 2003 (Actual)	FY 2004 (Enacted)	FY 2005 (Budget)
Department of Agriculture	1,176	828	737
Department of Commerce	326	250	308
Department of Energy	5	9	9
Department of Labor	1	1	1
Department of State	146	155	151
Department of Transportation	0	0	0
Department of the Treasury	3	3	3
Agency for International Development	NA	NA	NA
Environmental Protection Agency	0	0	0
Export-Import Bank	578	73	200
Overseas Private Investment Corporation	(239)	(199)	(187)
Small Business Administration	6	8	12
Trade and Development Agency	58	50	50
U.S. Trade Representative	35	42	40
Totals	2,334	1,419	1,511

Notes:

Totals do not include the Overseas Private Investment Corporation.

Amounts may be restated in the future to reflect new data or definitions. Figures may include administrative expenses, transfers, or other adjustments.

Figures for the U.S. Agency for International Development (USAID) do not appear in this table, as USAID activities support trade promotion indirectly through broad economic growth and reform, unlike other activities that more directly fund trade finance or promotion.

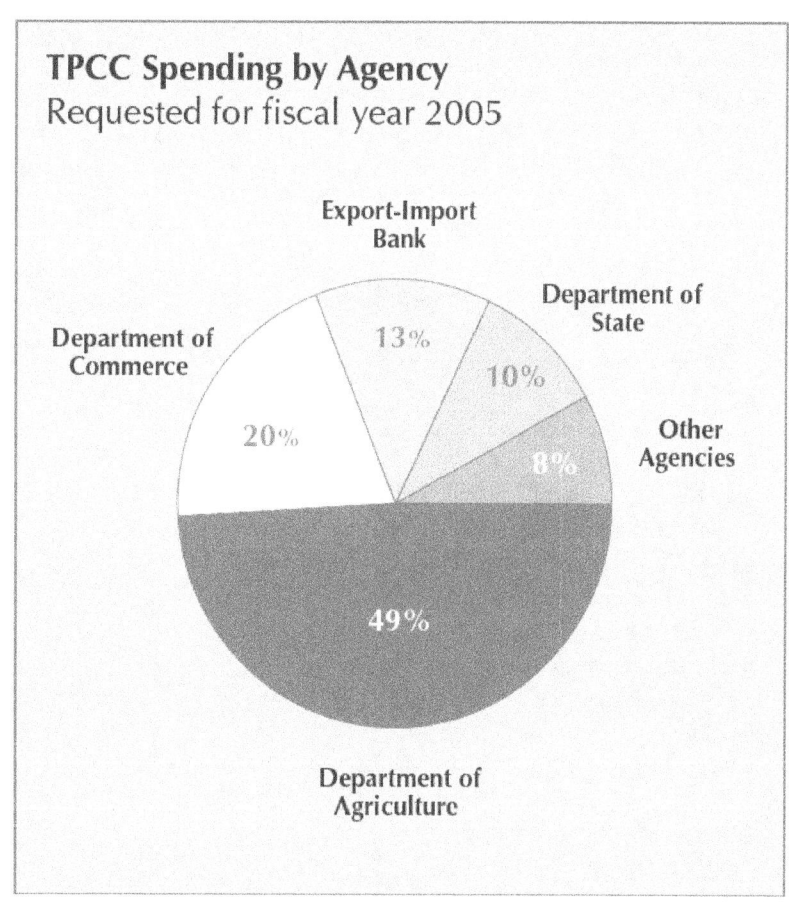

TPCC Spending by Agency
Requested for fiscal year 2005

Appendix C: Abbreviations and Acronyms

AGOA	African Growth and Opportunity Act
APEC	Asia-Pacific Economic Cooperation forum
ATO	Agricultural Trade Office (USDA)
BANOBRAS	Banco Nacional de Obras y Servicios Publicos, S.N.C. (development bank, Mexico)
BEA	Bureau of Economic Analysis (DOC)
BISNIS	Business Information Service for the Newly Independent States (ITA)
CAFTA	U.S. Central American Free Trade Agreement
CCC	Commodity Credit Corporation (USDA)
CCPIT	China Council for Promotion of International Trade
CDB	China Development Bank
CEEBIC	Central and Eastern Europe Business Information Center (ITA)
CITD	Centers for International Trade Development (California)
CPA	Coalition Provisional Authority
CS	Commercial Service (ITA)
DMIA	Data Management Improvement Act
DOC	U.S. Department of Commerce
DOT	U.S. Department of Transportation
ECA	export credit agency
EBRD	European Bank for Reconstruction and Development
EU	European Union
E-TAP	Export Trade Assistance Partnership (SBA)
Ex-Im Bank	Export-Import Bank of the United States
FAS	Foreign Agricultural Service (USDA)
FEED	front-end engineering and design
FSI	Foreign Service Institute
FTA	free trade agreement
FTAA	Free Trade Area of the Americas
FY	fiscal year
GDITT	Georgia Department of Industry, Trade, and Tourism
GDP	gross domestic product
GSP	Generalized System of Preferences
IA	Import Administration (ITA)
ICRAS	U.S. Interagency Country Risk Assessment System
IT	information technology
ITA	International Trade Administration (DOC)
JCCT	Joint Commission on Commerce and Trade
MAC	Market Access and Compliance (ITA)
MAS	Manufacturing and Services (ITA)
MDB	multilateral development banks
MOFCOM	Ministry of Commerce (China)
MOU	memorandum of understanding
NAB	National Association of Broadcasters
NAFIN	Nacional Financiera S.N.A. (development bank, Mexico)
NAM	National Association of Manufacturers
NASBITE	North American Small Business International Trade Educators
NPES	The Association for Suppliers of Printing, Publishing, and Converting Technologies

OECD	Organization for Economic Cooperation and Development
OPIC	Overseas Private Investment Corporation
OTTI	Office of Travel and Tourism Industries (ITA)
SBA	U.S. Small Business Administration
SBAC	Small Business Assistance Corporation
SBC	Small Business Center (OPIC)
SBDC	Small Business Development Center (SBA)
SEED	Support for East European Democracy Act of 1989
SME	small- and medium-sized enterprise
STAR	Secure Trade in the APEC Region
TBI	Trade Bank of Iraq
TIC	Trade Information Center (ITA)
TP	Trade Promotion (ITA)
TPC	Tourism Policy Council
TPCC	Trade Promotion Coordinating Committee
TTSA	Travel and Tourism Satellite Accounts
UN	United Nations
USAID	U.S. Agency for International Development
USDA	U.S. Department of Agriculture
USEAC	U.S. Export Assistance Center (CS, Ex-Im Bank, SBA)
USTDA	U.S. Trade and Development Agency
USTR	Office of the U.S. Trade Representative
WFP	World Food Program
WTO	World Trade Organization